ECHOES OF UTOPIA

Echoes of Utopia

Studies in the legacy of Marx

MICHAEL FULLER
Bolton Institute, UK

Routledge
Taylor & Francis Group
LONDON AND NEW YORK

First published 2000 by Ashgate Publishing

Reissued 2019 by Routledge
2 Park Square, Milton Park, Abingdon, Oxon, OX14 4RN
52 Vanderbilt Avenue, New York, NY 10017

Routledge is an imprint of the Taylor & Francis Group, an informa business

A Library of Congress record exists under LC control number:

ISBN 13: 978-1-138-74114-0 (hbk)
ISBN 13: 978-1-138-74111-9 (pbk)
ISBN 13: 978-1-315-18301-5 (ebk)

Contents

Preface

Echoes of Utopia sets out to explore the question of the continuing relevance of Marx's thought.

Chapter 1 opens with a conceptual analysis of Marx's "organic composition of capital" idea. It is critical of this idea, as well as of the related ideas of the labour theory of value and surplus value. The analysis ends by concluding that what truth there is in the organic composition of capital idea derives its forces from Marx's more fundamental ideas about overproduction, underconsumption and crises.

Chapter 2 proceeds with a more socio-economic historical analysis of Marx's overproduction/underconsumption ideas in the light of the New Right, globalization, and the "crisis of Keynesianism". It concludes that Marx's ideas on this score still have contemporary relevance, but three substantial areas of doubt remain for the Marxist project: (a) the controversy of market versus planning; (b) the utopian/scientific socialism debate ("mere dreaming" versus "real historical forces"); (c) ecological limits and constraints in relation to the "removal of scarcity".

Chapter 3 proceeds to partially address these doubts through the work of Joseph Schumpeter with his ambivalent attitude to Marx. It concentrates very much on the centralization aspect and the economic dimension.

Chapter 4 continues to address these doubts through the work of Simone Weil with her equally ambivalent attitude to Marx. It concentrates very much on the decentralization aspect and the political/moral dimension.

Chapter 5 tries to pull all the preceding threads together. It identifies "decentralization within centralization" as one of Marx's leading ideas in both the political and economic spheres. It tries to assess the strengths and weaknesses of Schumpeter's and Weil's analyses. It continues with an imaginary conversation with the "spectre of Marx" concerning the nature of the good society. Finally, it tries to address the question of "real historical forces" in the contemporary world.

I would like to acknowledge some of the many people, past and present, who have had some impact on this book: Mike Walsh, Malcolm Pittock, the late Myron Kofman, Gerry Rowley, Karen Mosses, Catherine Stott, David Lamb, Rob Campbell, Mark Price, Martin Thomasson.

1 Marx's Bad Idea: The Organic Composition of Capital

Introduction

Why is Marx's technical idea about the "organic composition of capital" so important? Because it is the constellation of all his key economic ideas: his theory of surplus value and exploitation, his explanation of where profits come from and what economic value is, and his explanation of why the rate of profit must inevitably fall, leading to severe crises within capitalism and its eventual collapse.

Why is the organic composition of capital a bad idea? Because (1) its underlying assumptions - the labour theory of value and profit stemming fundamentally from the exploited surplus value of living labour - can be criticized as dubious or vacuous; and because (2) even if we accept its underlying assumptions as correct, it can be argued that these assumptions do not necessarily lead to where Marx thinks they must lead: to a falling rate of profit and the collapse of capitalism. Even more tellingly, it can be argued that Marx himself in the *Grundrisse* argues against his own organic composition of capital idea. The reason that he does not seem to realize that he is arguing against himself is because he mixes up there his argument about the organic composition of capital with two other arguments: his good idea about the tendencies to overproduction/underconsumption crises within capitalism, and his more contentious idea that the productive fruits of science and technology stem from "social labour" as a whole, and therefore ought rightly to belong to society as a whole (rather than, say, to the individuals who invented them or the individuals who put up the cash to make them industrial realities).

In what follows, I divide the discussion into five parts:
(1) I shall try to explain what the organic composition of capital is and how it connects with Marx's other key ideas. (2) I shall examine criticisms which reject the underlying assumptions about the labour theory of value

and surplus value. (3) I shall examine criticisms which accept the labour theory of value and surplus value but nevertheless reject the consequences that are supposed to flow from the resulting argument about the organic composition of capital: a falling rate of profit leading to capitalism's collapse. (4) I shall examine the *Grundrisse* argument about automation. (5) Finally, I shall try to assess what worth remains of the whole idea of the organic composition of capital.

I The organic composition of capital

According to Marx, the economic worth of any commodity - i.e., its price or exchange-value - must be determined by some objective standard which is common to all commodities. Otherwise, the economic value of commodities would be subject to the chaos of relative and varying individual preferences regarding use-value. For example, a bottle of whiskey might have enormous use-value to an alcoholic but nil use-value to a teetotaller. So, to avoid chaos, a common criterion must be found which measures the worth of every good (a standard of value) and also the relative worth of every good in relation to other goods (a measure of exchange). So far as Marx can see, the most fruitful avenue for finding such a common criterion that will determine the economic value of every product is to be found in the amount of labour that has entered into its production. Hence the Labour Theory of Value. Marx explains it thus:

> A use-value, or useful article, therefore, has value only because human labour in the abstract has been embodied or materialized in it. How, then, is the magnitude of this value to be measured? Plainly, by the quantity of the value creating substance, the labour, contained in the article. The quantity of labour, however, is measured by its duration, and labour-time in its turn finds its standard in weeks, days, and hours. [1]

By such means, then, we can arrive at something like the "intrinsic value" of a commodity, and its "proper price" or "just price" - an idea with clear moral overtones.

Marx then proceeds to explore the implications of this in regard to capitalism. If everything sells at the "proper price" determined by the amount of labour that has gone into it, then it would be impossible to realize any excess as profit, and impossible for capitalism to function. Yet profit and capitalism exist. How is this possible? Marx explains the anomaly by arguing that there is *one* commodity - living labour - which does *not* sell at its proper price, and therefore living labour must be the source of profit. The capitalist gets a free lunch out of the worker by extracting (or exploiting) the worker's surplus value. So here is the case where the proper price is not paid to the worker, who is forced to work more hours (and so to realize more value as profit for the capitalist) than he or she is paid for. Here is the unique instance where use-value does not equal exchange-value, since the capitalist gets more use-value (work) out of the worker than the exchange-value (wages) which he pays the worker. Hence profits.

It is easy to see why this idea is compelling, since it is based on the paradigm of the free lunch that is obtained by exploiting slave labour - the most naked example of exploiting someone by getting more out of them than you give back to them. The "wage slave" in capitalist society, argues Marx, is in an analogous position, in spite of pious cant about freedom of contract: forced, by dire necessity of the existing conditions of ownership, to "freely accept the contract" of working more hours than he or she is paid for.

The next step is to argue that the best way to maximize profit (and even to ensure survival, given the competitive pressures on capitalists) is to maximize productivity of workers. Thanks to the wonders of technology, one of the most effective ways of doing this is to introduce "labour-saving machinery". This brings us to the heart of our discussion. The organic composition of capital can be defined as the relative amounts of "constant capital" or "c" (raw materials and machinery) and of variable capital or "v" (living labour) that are involved in any process of production. Where the relative amount of c involved is high in relation to the amount of v involved, we are said to have a high organic composition of capital.

The problem, as Marx sees it, is that introducing labour-saving machinery to make workers more productive has an inevitable tendency to reduce the rate of profit. Why? Because surplus value, on Marx's premisses, only comes from living labour; no surplus value can come from raw materials and machinery. So he tells us:

> Therefore the means of production can never add more value to the product than they themselves possess independently of the process in which they assist. However useful a given kind of raw material, or a machine, or other means of production may be, though it may cost £150, or say 500 days' labour, yet it

cannot, under any circumstances, add to the value of the product more than £150.......

The property therefore which labour power in action, living labour, possesses of preserving value at the same time that it adds to it, is a gift of Nature which costs the labourer nothing but which is very advantageous to the capitalist inasmuch as it preserves the value of his capital. [2]

The essence of the organic composition of capital argument can be further clarified by the following three extracts:

Now what higher productivity tends to mean is that the amount of plant and equipment each worker sets in motion increases....

But this development causes severe problems for the capitalist. For it means that he has to lay out an ever larger amount of money on plant and equipment for every worker he employs. Yet it is the *worker* who is the source of the capitalist's profits - his or her labour produces that surplus value above his or her wages. So the cost of investments rises faster than the profits squeezed out of the workforce. In other words, the return that the capitalist gets on his investment, the rate of profit, falls. [3]

Capitalists, in Marx's model, have both to produce surplus value from exploitation in the process of production and realize it by selling their products at a profit in the market. This leads to a contradiction between keeping workers' wages down and expecting them to be able to afford to buy their own increased production. The problem is only solved so long as purchasing power, including credit, just rises to match increased productivity. But there is a further and more serious contradiction in the capitalist system, according to Marx. As more and more capital is introduced with each unit of labour, changing what Marx called the organic composition of capital, it will be more and more difficult to maintain the rate of surplus per worker and so profit rates will tend to fall. [4]

For as he [the capitalist] substitutes machines for men, he is simultaneously substituting nonprofitable means of production for profitable ones. Remember that in Marx's model of an ideal capitalist world, no one makes a profit by merely sharp bargaining. Whatever a machine will be worth to a capitalist, you can be sure that he paid full value for it. If a machine will yield ten thousand dollars' worth of value over its whole life, our capitalist was presumably charged the full ten thousand dollars in the first place. It is only from his living labour that he can realize a profit, only from the unpaid-for hours of surplus working time. Hence, when he reduces the number or proportion of workers, he is killing the goose that lays the golden egg. [5]

Here, then, we have the essence of the idea: a typical example of the kind of dialectical thinking which Marx took over from Hegel, an example of what Hegel grandly called "an emergent yet antithetical result". All unintended, the attempt to maximize profit via machinery has the unforeseen result of minimizing it, so creating the conditions for a descending spiral of economic and social chaos, misery and unrest, culminating in revolution.

But is it a good idea?

II Criticisms of the labour theory of value and surplus value

Before we begin, we should mention an empirical question. *Does* the rate of profit in fact show tendencies to fall? Unfortunately, it is very hard to get clear and definite answers on this score. Some claim that the rate of profit has shown a tendency to fall, so confirming Marx's predictions based on his organic composition of capital idea. Others claim that it has not shown any such tendency, so refuting Marx's predictions. Yet others argue that while capitalism has shown a tendency to falling rates of profit *within* business cycles, it shows no such tendency absolutely. Yet others again argue that, even if it were conclusively shown that capitalism does have a tendency towards absolutely falling rates of profit, this would in no way conclusively prove Marx's organic composition of capital idea, since the causes of the fall in the rate of profit might lie elsewhere. The best that we can conclude is perhaps that empirically the issue is not settled and that, even if it were settled affirmatively, this would still only provide evidence rather than conclusive proof in favour of Marx's organic composition of capital idea.

Part I has shown that the logic of Marx's argument is as follows: his arguments about the organic composition of capital and falling rates of profit are deductions from his arguments about surplus value; his arguments about surplus value are in turn deductions from his arguments about the labour theory of value. Unsurprisingly, then, a number of Marx's critics have gone straight for the jugular and aimed their attacks at what they see as simultaneously being the pivot and yet also the weakest point of Marx's economic theory: the labour theory of value.

These criticisms have been various though often interconnected. I think we can usefully distinguish three main strands of criticism. (1) The labour theory of value is dubious. (2) The labour theory of value is not so much dubious as metaphysical and vacuous, and perhaps amounts to little more than an arbitrary definition of value which Marx then uncritically adopts as an axiom from which he deduces results such as the idea of surplus value, the organic composition of capital, and the falling rate of profit. (3) The labour theory of value, whatever merit it might have as a philosophical and moral vision of socialism and justice, fares badly when subjected to the pragmatic test of how well it functions as an "analytic tool" in economic practice. When it comes to analyzing phenomena such as prices, it is argued, the labour theory of value is of far less use as an instrument for economists than subsequent theories of value such as the marginal utility theory. In comparison, the labour theory of value is a clumsy instrument and in order to try and close the gap between his economic theory and economic reality, Marx is forced to resort to some fairly circuitous reasoning and *ad hoc* hypothesizing. Since Marx was anxious to be seen not merely as another moral crusader or "utopian socialist", but as a "scientific socialist" whose theories could explain the minutiae of economic phenomena, the charge that the labour theory of value is in many respects a poor tool in economic analysis is not an insignificant matter.

The three strands of criticism mentioned above are all interconnected in the sense that it is quite possible for a critic to argue that the labour theory of value is dubious because it is vacuous and arbitrary, and that its vacuity and arbitrariness are shown by its deficiencies (in some, not all, respects) as a practical tool of economic analysis.

It might still be objected that "bourgeois economics", in refusing to accept Marx's version of the labour theory of value and surplus value, has robbed itself of the ability to explain the phenomena of *profit* and *value* and therefore deserves to be taken less seriously than Marxism as an economic philosophy. But this is surely a weak argument. Profit can be accounted for within a different explanatory schema (although admittedly a schema that does not decisively settle the issue of what is to count as "fair shares"). So one of the founding fathers of neo-classical economic theory, Alfred Marshall, criticized Marx in the following way:

> It is not true that the spinning of yarn in a factory, after allowance has been made for the wear-and-tear of the machinery, is the product of the labour of the operatives. It is the product of their labour, together with that of the employer and subordinate managers, and of the capital employed; and that capital itself is the product of labour and waiting; and therefore the spinning is the product of labour of many kinds, and of waiting. If we admit that it is the product of labour

> alone, and not of labour and waiting, we can no doubt be compelled by inexorable logic to admit that there is no justification of interest, the reward of waiting; for the conclusion is implied in the premiss. [6]

When it comes to the problem of explaining what economic value essentially is, it could be argued that no theory of value has been able to provide a convincing and comprehensive account of this elusive and multi-faceted phenomenon, and that, perhaps, after all, it is something of a philosophical pseudo-problem. It may be - as Wittgenstein and some pragmatist philosophers argue about essences in general - that there is no "intrinsic essence" of economic value. This is not the same thing as arguing that market prices arrived at by supply and demand are all there is to say about economic value and "just price". For to say that would only be to reintroduce a notion of the intrinsic essence of economic value surreptitiously. It is rather to say that the phenomenon of economic value (and the phenomena of "just price" and "fair shares" which are derived from it) may just be eternally morally and politically controversial - incapable of being resolved from the ground up by economic theory, whether in the form of the idea of market-clearing price mechanisms of marginal utility theory or the labour theory of value of Marx.

The above kinds of criticism of the labour theory of value - its dubiousness, its vacuity and its difficulties in practical application - are spelled out further in the following extracts:

> In the first volume of *Capital* Marx argued that as profit is created solely by surplus value, and as labour is the sole value-producing agency, the rate of profit will depend upon what he calls 'the organic composition of capitals', that is, the proportion of labour (variable capital) to machinery (constant capital) employed in a given undertaking; and that it will thus tend to fall in proportion as technological improvements lead to the employment of less labour. Yet although this conclusion logically followed from his premisses, it was demonstrably false in practice. Marx was aware of the difficulty ... But he did not face it at the time, and set it aside for further treatment. There the matter rested until 1883, when he died....
>
> The [solution] was, indeed, eagerly awaited, but when it appeared in the third volume [of *Capital*] it caused widespread disillusionment. For it was now contended that although the rate of profit did depend on the relation of variable to constant capital if the whole capital of the world was taken into account (and of this no proof was given), this did not apply to the profits of particular businesses, which tended to equalize themselves according to the state of trade.

As Joan Robinson points out, Marx's demonstration simply amounts to the tautology that if wages are constant (and elsewhere he denies that they are) the rate of profit will fall as capital per man increases......

Actually, he is ultimately driven to admit that exchange value is governed by the market, that is, by the law of supply and demand, which makes nonsense of his theory that it is derived from labour only. [7]

Certainly the moral effect of the overwhelming first volume of *Das Kapital* is likely to be weakened by an acquaintance with its successors. If all value is created by labour only in some metaphysical sense, then there may be more in those utility theories of value which Marxists regard as capitalist frauds than we had formerly been willing to admit. If it is possible for values to be reckoned as Marx reckoned them in units of abstract labour power, why was it not possible - what Marx had denied - to reckon them in units of an abstract utility? - especially when the supposed value of labour seems to have nothing to do with fixing prices, whereas demand of the consumer obviously has.

But the truth is that all such theories are incomplete: real prices are the results of situations much more complex than any of these formulas, and complicated by psychological factors which economists seldom take into account. The economist tends to imagine that value ... is something mainly created by the group to which he belongs or whose apologist he aims to be. The stupider type of old-fashioned manufacturer was practically under the impression that he was creating both the product and the labour by supplying the brains and the capital which gave the factory hand his opportunity to work. The Fabian Socialists represented the middle-class British consumer and they believed that the human being as consumer rather than as farm-labourer or factory hand determined the value of commodities by his demand for them. Karl Marx, who was not only on the side of the worker but wanted to see him inherit the earth, asserted that all value was created by labour. [8]

The central difficulty ... is the relation of values to prices. It has already been pointed out that for Marx the value of a commodity is *defined* in terms of embodied labour; this disposes of the question whether or not his value theory is 'wrong' - a pseudo-problem on which both his followers and his critics subsequently wasted a good deal of effort. The relevant question is whether on his assumptions it is possible to account for the movement of (long-range equilibrium) prices and profits; and the candid answer must be that, though not impossible in principle, the operation is so involved, and requires so many auxiliary hypotheses, as to be very nearly self-defeating in practice ....

Marx sets out by laying down the general rule that commodities tend to exchange at prices which correspond to their (embodied) values. 'Price is the money-name of the labour realised in a commodity.' (*Capital*, I, p. 74.) Temporary deviations from this rule are to be regarded as infractions of a general law which determines the exchange of commodities. In Volume III this principle is qualified by the admission that - account being taken of different capital-labour ratios in different industries, as well as the prevalence of a uniform rate of profit established by competition - commodities do not in fact exchange in accordance with embodied labour values, but rather according to 'prices of production', i.e., monetary costs plus an average profit. Whether one regards this admission as a fatal contradiction of the basic law laid down in Volume I (as did Bohm-Bawerk and others), or whether one regards it as a sensible qualification of a theoretical 'first approximation' whose significance is not diminished thereby, must ultimately depend on what one expects a theory of value to do. If one's interest is focused on a sociological explanation of the genesis and operation of capitalism, there is no particular reason why one should not employ the Marxian apparatus, since its conceptual tools are evidently suited to an approach which treats the accumulation of capital as the central mainspring of the entire process. If one believes that a theory of value must justify itself by enabling economists to derive prices from values, it is hard to see what useful purpose is served by trying to salvage a theoretical model which makes such an operation impossibly difficult. [9]

I conclude this section with an argument designed to show that constant capital (machinery) is just as capable as variable capital (living labour) of producing surplus value.

Suppose an entrepreneur builds an automatic crow-scarer for £1000. But the machine has the ability to perform, throughout its useful life, the equivalent of £3000 worth of the work of living labour (i.e., what it would cost a farmer to employ living labour to perform the same work that is done by the robot).

Now it seems on the Marxist analysis that the firm that makes the machine should sell it not for the £1000 (e.g., production costs) but for £3000 (e.g., real use to farmer and the same value as employing waged labour to do the work). Since the idea of the labour "locked up" or "embodied" in a machine seems ambiguous within the Marxist scheme when applied to robots. It seems to refer both to (a) "proper price" determined by the labour that goes into the machine's construction and (b) "proper price" determined by the equivalent amount of work-if-done-by-living-labour that the machine can produce over its effective life-span. It must mean (b) as well as (a), since, if it only meant (a), this would be tantamount to conceding that constant capital (machines) can produce surplus value.

But a digression into marginal economics shows us the fallacy of this: if the firm tried to sell at £3000, it would find no takers, since it would not be worth any farmer "clearing the market" at this price (at least, not unless he was stupendously silly or just happened to have an obsessive love of gadgets). Hence the firm would have to reduce the price - say, to £2000 - so that a "market-clearing price" is achieved that is of mutual benefit to both the producing firm (which easily covers its costs) and the farmer (who also easily achieves a profitable outcome).

This example is intended to show that *robots* (capital goods which involve *no* interaction with living labour) *can produce surplus value.* In this case, 'robots' have the same functions that Marx ascribes to living labour alone: what it costs to produce/reproduce them (exchange-value) is less than the work (use-value) that they can achieve for the capitalist. And what applies to robotics applies also to capital goods which do still involve some interaction with living labour. It is just that, given the Marxist dogma or definition that only living labour can produce surplus value, it is necessary to reinterpret the realities of what happens when mechanical diggers replace an army of navvies by declaring that the profits made result from the surplus value of the few remaining workers rather than from the contribution of the workers *plus* the contribution of the machines which make them so productive.

Nor will it help here to evasively argue, as Michael Harrington tries to:

> In the calculated oversimplification of his [Marx's] basic analyses - which generations have mistaken for a flawed description of the real world - it was assumed that raw materials, machines, and finance were all exchanged according to their value, and that sellers charged buyers a fair price. Where, then, was the source of profit? In the labor-market. [10]

For if Marx's "calculated oversimplification" does successfully reveal the way that profits are gained by capitalists from their workers, by the same stroke it successfully conceals the way that profits are also gained by capitalists from capital goods, ideas, and organization. Calling it a "calculated oversimplification" or "heuristic device" will not obscure the fact that it *is* a "flawed description of the real world" of business and industry. What Marx successfully conceals here is what Buckminster Fuller called the ability of technology and human ingenuity to do "more with less". Or, rather, Marx *does* recognize this ability of technology, but theorizes in such a way as to make it impossible for *capitalists* to reap any lasting benefit from this ability. This benefit must be reserved for communism.

Nor will it do more than qualify the argument slightly to declare, as Joseph Schumpeter acutely does:

> It is sufficient that ... the profit of every individual plant is incessantly being threatened by actual or potential competition from new commodities or methods of production which sooner or later will turn it into a loss. So we get the driving force required and even an analogon to Marx's proposition that constant capital does not produce surplus value - for no individual assemblage of capital goods remains a source of surplus gains forever - without having to rely on those parts of his argument which are of doubtful validity. [11]

What can be said, however, is that, if generalized, macro-economic problems may arise due to the rise of "technological unemployment" in my example leading to overproduction/underconsumption problems and hence a decline in the rate of profit. This is Marx's good idea - perhaps more relevant today than ever. But it is a separate argument from the one about the organic composition of capital.

III Criticisms concerning the falling rate of profit

In Part II, I raised various doubts both about Marx's labour theory of value and about the logically connected thesis that surplus value stemmed from variable capital (or living labour) alone. In Part III, I am going to argue that, even if one accepts Marx's labour theory of value and his surplus value idea, there is no necessary consequence of a falling rate of profit due to a changed organic composition of capital.

As George Lichteim puts it:

> That there was a long-run tendency for the rate of profit on capital to fall, was generally accepted by economists in Marx's time. His originality consisted in linking this prospect with what he termed the organic composition of capital, i.e., the ratio of constant (non-wage) to variable (wage) capital. Competition among capitalists, he held, would, via technical progress and capital accumulation, necessarily tend to enhance the proportion of embodied to living labour, or in different terms: raise the amount of capital per man employed; and

> since constant capital produced no additional surplus value, there would be a tendency for the share of profit to fall, assuming the rate of surplus value (or rate of exploitation) to remain unchanged. Marx took due note of countervailing tendencies such as increasing productivity of labour, but seems to have felt that on balance these could only slow down the fall in the ratio of surplus-value to embodied value. Thus a gradual decline in the rate of profit was postulated as an abstract tendency (or 'absolute law'), while the question to what extent it could be temporarily counteracted by forces working in the opposite direction was left open. [12]

This "abstract tendency" soon hardens into an article of faith for a certain kind of Marxist, in spite of the fact that, as Lichteim says:

> The whole conception is clearly abstract and depends (even if one accepts the Marxian proposition about surplus-value) on a balance of conflicting tendencies which might equally well operate in the other direction; and the most one can say of the theorem [of a fall in the rate of profit due to a changed organic composition of capital] is that it has not been (and probably cannot be) positively disproved. So far as the statistical evidence goes ... capital has consistently grown faster than the labour force; in some decades almost twice as fast. But since productivity per worker rose by approximately the same amount ... capital per worker did not grow in *value* terms, hence there was no reason why (on the Marxian assumption) profits should have declined. [13]

Of course, it is always possible for the Marxist to argue that, even if higher productivity per worker has staved off the tendency to a falling rate of profit, this is only because more surplus value is extracted from the worker who is consequently more exploited than ever. But this is to rather confuse together the technical and moral meanings of 'exploitation'. Technically, it may well be that a well-paid worker in an automated industry with lavish welfare schemes is more exploited than a Roman galley slave, since the modern worker may yield more surplus value. But morally, or in terms of human suffering, it is surely clear enough that the Roman slave is the more exploited.

Anyway, the point to be proved was that higher productivity per worker could not permanently postpone a fall in the rate of profit due to a changed organic composition of capital. And it has not been proved, even assuming the truth of the labour theory of value and surplus value. True, as Lichteim says, it could probably never be disproved either, since it is always possible to maintain that, even if the tendency to a falling rate of profit has not happened yet, it will happen tomorrow.

IV The *Grundrisse* argument about automation

In a prophetic passage of the *Grundrisse* - often seen as his rough draft for *Capital* - Marx tells us:

> to the degree that large industry develops, the creation of real wealth comes to depend less on labour time and on the amount of labour employed than on the power of the agencies set in motion during labour time, whose 'powerful effectiveness' is itself in turn out of all proportion to the direct labour time spent on their production, but depends rather on the general state of science and on the progress of technology, or the application of this science to production ... Labour no longer appears so much to be included within the production process; rather the human being comes to relate more as a watchman and regulator to the production process itself. No longer does the worker insert a modified natural thing as middle link between the object and himself; rather, he inserts the process of nature, transformed into an industrial process, as a means between himself and inorganic nature, mastering it. He steps to the side of the production process instead of being its chief actor. In this transformation, it is neither the direct human labour he himself performs, nor the time during which he works, but rather the appropriation of his own general productive power, his understanding of nature and his mastery over it by virtue of his presence as a social body - it is, in a word, the development of the social individual which appears as the great foundation-stone of production and of wealth ... As soon as labour in the direct form has ceased to be the great well-spring of wealth, labour time ceases and must cease to be its measure, and hence exchange value [must cease to be the measure] of use value. [14]

Michael Harrington interprets this passage in the following way:

> Capitalist socialization, Marx wrote, must eventually put science to work in the production process so that workers would simply be the 'watchers and regulators' of the system, not its drudges. That same development would, by making the individual in charge of automated machinery so unbelievably productive, totally undercut the labour basis of value. What rational connection could there be between pay and output when a single person could 'produce' what once had taken a thousand, or ten thousand, workers? Marx did not repeat

this argument in *Das Kapital* (although I think it continues to be present implicitly in his discussion of free time).[15]

Actually, there seem to be two ways in which Marx's passage can be taken. Either as Harrington interprets it, that is, in terms of the enormous productivity of labour (in which case it falls prey to the kind of criticisms made by Lichteim as outlined in Part III); or in terms of the enormous productivity of automated machinery itself (in which case it falls prey to the kind of criticism outlined in Part II - a "mechanical slave" may have the same propensity to producing surplus value as a human one, since its use-value to the capitalist is more than the cost (exchange-value) of its construction). Since, on either interpretation, it would seem to follow that there is nothing in automation *per se* which need be damaging to capitalism, this may be one reason why Marx did not repeat the argument in *Capital.* Perhaps he came to realize that the *Grundrisse* argument actually seems to undermine one pillar of his theory: the organic composition of capital leading to a falling rate of profit idea.

However, in the *Grundrisse* itself, Marx seems to feel that his speculations on automation actually support the organic composition of capital/falling rate of profit idea. For he goes on to say:

> Capital itself is the moving contradiction, in that it presses to reduce labour time to a minimum, while it posits labour time, on the other side, as sole measure and source of wealth. Hence it diminishes labour time in the necessary form so as to increase it in the superfluous form; hence posits the superfluous in growing measure as a condition - question of life or death - for the necessary.[16]

And again:

> What capital adds is that it increases the surplus labour time of the mass by all the means of art and science, because its wealth consists directly in the appropriation of surplus labour time ... It is thus, despite itself, instrumental in creating the means of social disposable time, in order to reduce labour time for the whole society to a diminishing minimum, and thus to free everyone's time for their own development. But its tendency always, on the one side, *to create disposable time, on the other, to convert it into surplus labour.* If it succeeds too well at the first, then it suffers from surplus production, and then necessary labour is interrupted, because no *surplus labour can be realized by capital.*[17]

If we take these three extracts from the *Grundrisse* as a whole, it seems to me that Marx is mixing together in a rather confused and confusing way three separate arguments: (1) his standard argument about the organic composition of capital/ falling rate of profit, derived from his labour theory of value and surplus value; (2) his excellent argument about tendencies to crises resulting from technological unemployment, overproduction and underconsumption; (3) a kind of moral argument to the effect that the fruits of automation should belong to the "social body" as a whole, since they are the product of the social body as a whole. The first argument we have already subjected to criticism; the second argument is good, but there is nothing necessary about it in regard to capitalism's demise, since it is always possible, in principle if not always in fact, to sustain consumption by creating jobs in new lines of demand for goods and services (an idea central to Schumpeter's ideas of the "creative destruction" of capitalism and presumably an article of faith of most market theorists); the third argument is at least contentious, since some would argue that the inventors, entrepreneurs, financiers, research institutes and corporations who make new techniques into industrial realities deserve more reward for their labours than an amorphous entity called the "social body".

V Conclusion

Finally, what worth, if any, is left of Marx's idea of the organic composition of capital? It is easy to point out its flaws. Fundamentally, Marx could be accused of committing something like the opposite of the fallacy first pointed out by David Hume. Hume famously remarked that he had observed that sometimes philosophers will begin by arguing that such and such *is* the case, and then, without any detectable logical connection, proceed to infer that, because such and such *is* (factually) the case, therefore it *ought* (evaluatively) to be the case. Hume's argument, further refined by G.E. Moore, came to be variously known as the Naturalistic Fallacy, the fallacy of arguing from an 'is' to an 'ought', and the fallacy of arguing from fact to value.

Marx could be accused of reversing this procedure and fallaciously arguing from an 'ought' to an 'is', or from the *ideal* capitalism of what Harrington called his "calculated oversimplification" that all commodities exchange according to the value of the labour that goes into making them to the real capitalism of market prices. From his *ideal* capitalism (which is to say, from the labour theory of value), he then fallaciously infers a number of consequences supposed to follow for the *real* capitalist world: namely, that the surplus value of living labour must be the real source of profit, that constant capital cannot produce profit, and that a high organic composition of capital must imply a falling rate of profit. Hence his difficulties in easily deriving (real) prices from his (ideal) values. Hence also his difficulties in satisfactorily explaining automation within his explanatory schema (since it would seem to have the same properties that Marx ascribes to living labour and so be capable of producing surplus value for capitalism).

Even so, it would be premature to dismiss the organic composition of capital idea completely. Firstly, as Joseph Schumpeter pointed out, even if we reject the labour theory of value, we are still left with a kind of "analogon" to Marx's organic composition of capital idea:

> the profit of every individual plant is incessantly being threatened by actual or potential competition... So we get ... an analogon to Marx's proposition that constant capital does not produce surplus value - for no individual assemblage of capital goods remains a source of surplus gains forever. [18]

Secondly, and most fundamentally of all, what truth there is in the organic composition of capital idea is intrinsically linked to Marx's argument about technological unemployment and overproduction/ underconsumption tendencies in capitalism. The connection is succinctly brought out by Andre Gorz in the following, with its echoes of Max Weber and Jurgen Habermas concerning "technical rationality", as well as of J.K. Galbraith's arguments in *The Affluent Society*:

> Economic rationality has never ... been *in the service* of any *determinate* goal. Its object is ... the maximization of the type of efficiency that it knows how to measure arithmetically. The main indicator of this efficiency is the rate of profit. And the rate of profit depends, in the last analysis, on the productivity of labour. The pursuit of an unlimited maximum of efficiency and profit would therefore demand the greatest possible growth of the productivity of labour and, as a result, of production. Increasing quantities of capital must be accumulated in machines that are both increasingly efficient and more numerous and this capital has to produce a return enabling the capitalist to install even more efficient machines, and so on.
>
> To make it worth investing increasing amounts of capital, it was clearly necessary that increasing production should find purchasers, and therefore that consumption should continue to expand well beyond the satisfaction of actually

felt needs ... But in this latter eventuality - the one which has in fact materialized - *consumption would have to be in the service of production.* [19]

We see here how the organic composition of capital idea is logically parasitic on the more fundamental idea of overproduction/ underconsumption tendencies within capitalism. The only way to make investment in machinery profitable (and so stave off Marx's argument about falling rate of profit due to high organic composition of capital) is to make mass consumption equal mass production. This mundane necessity to cover the costs of production by sales obviously holds whether one accepts Marx's arguments about the labour theory of value and surplus value or not. And, within a capitalist framework, the only acceptable way to make mass consumption equal mass production is to manufacture wants and to engage in unnecessary production of goods and services in order to provide the wherewithal (jobs, incomes) to sustain mass consumption. As a result, capitalism either tends to stifle the full potential of forces of production or to maximize them crookedly through the production of relatively superfluous goods and services for those with the money to pay for them. Or, viewed globally, it does both at once. So hairdressers in the UK have the wherewithal to pay for CD players, fashionable clothes and cosmetic surgery while villagers in Africa may still lack clean drinking water or sufficient food.

This is Marx's good idea.

Notes

1. Karl Marx (Capital I, 1:1), *Marx on Economics*, ed. Robert Freedman, Penguin, 1962, p. 30.
2. K. Marx (Capital I, 8), Ibid., pp. 67-68.
3. Alex Callinicos, *The Revolutionary Road to Socialism*, Socialist Worker's Party, 1984, pp. 16-17.
4. Michael Barratt Brown, *Models in Political Economy*, Penguin, 1990, pp. 87-88.
5. Robert Heilbroner, *The Worldly Philosophers*, Penguin, 1953, p. 122.
6. Alfred Marshall, *Principles of Economics*, Vol. I, Macmillan (London), 1961, p. 5-7.
7. R.N. Carew Hunt, *The Theory and Practice of Communism*, Penguin, 1950, pp. 86-87.
8. Edmund Wilson, *To the Finland Station*, W.H. Allen, 1960, p. 302.

9. George Lichteim, *Marxism*, Routledge, 1961, pp. 180-181.
10. Michael Harrington, *Socialism: Past and Future*, Pluto Press, 1993, p. 221.
11. Joseph Schumpeter, *Capitalism, Socialism and Democracy*, George Allen & Unwin, 1987, p. 33.
12. G. Lichteim, *Marxism*, p. 187.
13. G. Lichteim, Ibid., p. 188.
14. K. Marx, *Grundrisse*, trans. M. Nicolaus, Allen Lane, 1973, pp. 704-705.
15. M. Harrington, *Socialism: Past and Future*, p. 116.
16. K. Marx, *Grundrisse*, p. 706.
17. K. Marx, Ibid., p. 708.
18. J. Schumpeter, *Capitalism, Socialism and Democracy*, p. 33.
19. Andre Gorz, *Critique of Economic Reason*, trans. G. Handyside and C. Turner, Verso, 1989, p. 114.

2 Marx's Good Idea: Overproduction, Underconsumption and Crises

Introduction

Today, more than ever, it is tantalising to read prophetic books of the H.G. Wells variety predicting technical utopias: creative leisure societies where "mechanical slaves" will do all or most of the work. Here, it would seem, is the best of all possible worlds: a leisure society of the many rather than the few, based on slave labour, yet without the need for any social conscience about the lot of the slaves.

Marx, too, obviously believed in this vision. If we ignore some of his more utopian pronouncements, such as the famous passage in *The German Ideology* where he claims rather improbably that a communist society will be able to dispense with specialisation and division of labour, leaving everybody free to do a bit of what they fancy as regards what necessary work remains - if we ignore that, then we are left with two main trends. Firstly, the technical utopian trend that, since the mechanical slaves will do much of the work, humans will be liberated for more leisure; secondly, the argument that, freed of capitalist pressures, what necessary work remains can be made more creative and pleasant. Both these trends are further reinforced by the Marxist argument that, free from the false consciousness induced by capitalism, communists will have enough sense to be able to distinguish between real needs and artificial wants, so eliminating the need for much superfluous production and work. True, the flip side of this coin, that communist society will be able to "boost the productive forces", so removing scarcity in regard to man's needs in a way unimaginable under capitalism (whose structural constraints must inhibit "the full potential of productive forces"), does not in itself promise a reduction in the need for work.

Marx of course held that none of the fruits of technological development could be realised within capitalism - or, at least, to the extent that they could be realised, they would be realised crookedly - so he presumably would not have been surprised that, in spite of the enormous productivity gains allowed by the "micro-chip revolution", the contemporary experience is all too often overwork, insecurity and stress for those "lucky enough to have jobs", while all too often the "leisure society" made possible by technological advances translates crookedly in real terms as the different kinds of financial stress and insecurity put upon those who are either underemployed (temporary, part-time workers) or unemployed. For these last two categories especially - the "lucky recipients" of this "leisure society" - the situation is further aggravated by the pressures which contemporary global capitalism passes on to national governments to reduce the costs of the welfare state.

Marx provided two basic explanations of why something like this was almost bound to happen. His first explanation was that a high organic composition of capital had tendencies towards a falling rate of profit; his second explanation was that capitalism tended towards ever worsening crises based on overproduction and underconsumption leading to a fall in the rate of profit. What truth there is in the organic composition of capital idea reduces to what truth there is in the more fundamental idea of crises due to overproduction and underconsumption. For the organic composition of capital idea boils down to the following simple proposition: business will be unable to recoup the costs of investment in productivity-enhancing technology unless it can sell all the (extra) product it produces by these means; but since, other things being equal, the very producers which it is replacing with machinery are also the consumers on whom it depends to buy its product, there will be inevitable tendencies to overproduction and underconsumption, markets will soon become "saturated", whether we are talking about existing product or new lines of product. As a result, capitalism must also have a tendency to "stifle the full potential of its productive forces", since, under capitalist conditions of exchange, there will not be enough people with enough income to buy the full product that can be (potentially but not actually) offered for consumption. So the result is a tendency to overcapacity within global capitalism, and of (actual) poverty in the midst of (potential) plenty.

In what follows, I divide the discussion into six parts: (1) Marx's Ideas on Overproduction, Underconsumption, and Crises; (2) The Keynesian Response: the Welfare State and the "Acceptable Face of Capitalism"; (3) The Affluent Society: Galbraith as Heretical Keynesian; (4) Inflation, Stagflation, Globalization, Automation; (5) The Implications for Keynesianism; (6) The Implications for Marxism.

I Marx on overproduction, underconsumption and crises

For Marx, it is inevitable that capitalism must invest in labour-saving machinery, displacing workers, since the conditions of capitalist production make this the only way to stay competitive. So he tells us:

> This is a law of capitalist production imposed by incessant revolution in the methods of production themselves, the resulting depreciation of existing capital, the general competitive struggle, and the necessity of improving the product and expanding the scale of production for the sake of self-preservation and on penalty of failure... But to the extent that the productive power develops, it finds itself at variance with the narrow basis on which the conditions of consumption rest. [1]

Later, he elaborates on why this must be so:

> as matters stand, the reproduction of the capitals invested in production depends largely upon the consuming power of the non-producing classes; while the consuming power of the labourers is handicapped partly by the laws of wages, partly by the fact that it can be exerted only so long as the labourers can be employed at a profit for the capitalist class. The last cause of all real crises always remains the poverty and restricted consumption of the masses as compared to the tendency of capitalist production to develop the productive forces in such a way that only the absolute consuming power of the entire society would be their limit. [2]

But, if the basic problem is one of insufficient demand due to poverty, then why cannot it be solved - and capitalism restored to a happy equilibrium - by simply redistributing wealth to allow of sufficient demand? For, as J.K.Galbraith sardonically observed:

> Since the government, for Marx, was the handmaiden of the bourgeoisie, there was small likelihood that it would be impelled to succour the unemployed by making jobs for them. But were it to do so the effect would only be to reduce the industrial reserve army, raise wage costs, and cause a depression. To correct the deficiency of purchasing power- the deficiency that kept workers from buying the products of their labour - by public measures to put more purchasing power in the hands of the people, as by spending for public works, would be futile for the same reasons .... this point is one of considerable importance to Marx and even more to his followers. Were it possible to prevent depressions by compensating for the deficient purchasing power of the worker with (say) public spending, then capitalism might be workable. Instead of a revolution, there would be a budget deficit. Every acute Marxian has seen the danger and denied the possibility of such an easy escape. In one of those developments which make economics such an engaging study in odd bedfellows, the Marxists have been joined in this contention by the most stalwart conservatives. [3]

And Marx does indeed close off such an "easy escape". He tells us:

> It is purely a tautology to say that crises are caused by the scarcity of solvent consumers, or of a paying consumption. The capitalist system does not know any other modes of consumption but a paying one, except that of the pauper or the 'thief'..... But if one were to attempt to clothe this tautology with a semblance of a profounder justification by saying that the working class receive too small a portion of their own product, and the evil would be remedied by giving them a larger share of it, or raising their wages, we should reply that crises are precisely always preceded by a period in which wages rise generally and the working class actually get a larger share..... From the point of view of the advocates of 'simple' (!) common sense, such a period should rather remove a crisis. It seems then that capitalist production comprises certain conditions which are independent of good or bad will and permit the working class to enjoy

that relative prosperity only momentarily, and at that always as a harbinger of a coming crisis. [4]

At this point in the argument, economic theory joins hands with economic history, since J.M. Keynes believed that he had discovered the "easy escape" in the form of budget deficit rather than a revolution. Historically, this ushered in the "never had it so good" years of the welfare state, the "acceptable face of capitalism", and the utopian aspirations of Galbraith's *The Affluent Society*, Anthony Crosland's *The Future of Socialism*, and Herbert Marcuse's *Eros* and *Civilisation.* But since it was followed by the period of Reagonomics, Thatcherism, monetarism, supply-side economics, globalization, the "internationalisation of capital", the "crisis of the welfare state" and the "collapse of Keynesianism", it could be that Marx maybe had a point after all.

It is to these matters that I turn now.

II The Keynesian response: the welfare state and "the acceptable face of capitalism"

Although Keynes seems to have regarded Marx as in many ways a defunct economist, it is obvious that Keynes shared with Marx the view that capitalism, left to itself, tends not towards the kind of optimum equilibrium theorised by J.B. Say's "law of markets", bût towards instability and crisis, boom and bust. (Or, at least, to the extent that Say's Law was correct, the equilibrium achieved could just as easily be at the trough of a self-perpetuating depression as at the peak of full employment of resources - a trickle of savings, a trickle of investment, a trickle of production and consumption). It is also obvious that Keynes agreed with Marx about underconsumption being "the last cause of all real crises". What Keynes essentially did as regards diagnosis was to add some extra refinements to Marx's overproduction/underconsumption account by highlighting the role of savings and investments in the dynamics of economic crisis. The point is well put by Michael Barratt Brown:

> In a boom he [Keynes] noted that the proportion of income going to savings

rose, so that there were more funds available for investment - by which he meant actual purchases of capital goods. For a time capital investment rose, but if consumption did not rise in line with this new capacity to produce goods, a crisis arose. Capital investment was suddenly stopped as stocks of unbought goods built up. There was nothing in the market model to ensure that the balance between savings and consumption was equal to the balance between investment in capital goods and the production of consumption goods. [5]

This, then, fundamentally, was Keynes's diagnosis of the Wall Street Crash of 1929 and the Great Depression of the 1930s, a diagnosis very much in the *spirit* of the Marxist one concerning overproduction/underconsumption and the "anarchy of production" of unfettered capitalism.

The real differences between Keynes and Marx appear when it comes to the question of prescription for the ills of capitalism. Marx believed that there was a fatal contradiction between the need for an unemployed "industrial reserve army" to keep wages and prices down (and profits up) and the incompatible need for high employment at good rates of pay to consume the full product (and keep profits up). Marx did not see how any juggling act within capitalism was capable of resolving this contradiction with its attendant crises and human misery. So eventually capitalism would have to go, to be replaced by a more rational system of economics.

To be fair, Keynes too could not see how any such juggling act was possible within existing capitalism. But he did believe it was possible within a modified form of capitalism, which would itself then constitute the more rational system of economics that appeared to be needed. I think it is fair to say that the essential features of this Keynesian model were as follows: (1) The government should intervene in such a way as to manage overall demand in the economy as a whole (the macro-economy), mainly through the operation of its fiscal policy (taxation, government spending and borrowing) and its monetary policy (interest rates, credit). (2) Meanwhile, the everyday activities of business people and workers and finance (the micro-economy) would be left free to operate along conventional market lines within the broad parameters set by governmental "demand-management" of the whole economy. (3) To cure a depression, government steps in to stimulate demand and employment by going into budget deficit. (4) As the economy responds to the injection of government demand, and the economy picks up, the government is able to recover its deficits via taxation, aiming towards a balanced budget. (5) If the economy shows signs of "overheating" due to too *much* inflation-inducing demand, the government reverses the policies it employed during depressions. Instead of stimulating demand by government spending, low taxation, and low interest rates, it dampens demand and inflation by cutbacks in government spending, high taxation, and high interest rates, aiming towards a budget surplus. (6) However - and here is the real magic of the scheme in theory - if the government gets its sums right and juggles all the variables effectively, "fine tuning" the economy, it will smooth out the worst excesses of booms and busts, inflationary "overheatings" and depressive slumps of the "business cycle", and the whole economy will operate on a more or less beatific upward curve: full employment, low inflation, sustained economic growth, some relatively painless redistribution of wealth. And these conditions are themselves the requirements for the moral crown of Keynesianism : the universal welfare state, "security from cradle to grave" for all citizens - "the acceptable face of capitalism".

The political and moral importance of the technical economic jugglings of Keynesianism are vividly brought out by George Dalton in the following extract:

> It was just like a child addicted to strawberry jam being told that jam is extraordinarily nutritious and prolongs life. The socialists had argued for a century that there were strong moral reasons to make the poor less poor and the rich less rich, to assure everyone a decent minimum income, and to provide a sufficiency of those life-giving services of health care, education and housing. Now Keynes told us there are hard-headed economic reasons for doing so. To redistribute income in favour of the poor is to assure a higher level of consumption spending - effective demand - out of any level of national income. For government to permanently increase its spending - effective demand - on health, education, and housing is to reduce the amount of private investment spending that must be forthcoming to sustain employment. [6]

Here, then, was Keynes' answer to Marx: wealth *could* be successfully redistributed within a modified capitalism; crises *could* be controlled; no fatal "inner contradictions" need be involved. Confidence in Keynesian solutions lasted well into the 1970s. But before turning to examine the loss of confidence in Keynesianism, I want to pause to consider the work of a "heretical Keynesian". An article of faith of orthodox Keynesians was that full employment was a desirable thing. J.K. Galbraith, good Keynesian though he was, dared to wonder why.

III The affluent society: Galbraith as heretical Keynesian

The Affluent Society, the book which first made J.K. Galbraith famous, was published in 1958, during the heyday of Keynesianism. Galbraith was enough of an orthodox Keynesian to have no doubts that Keynes had provided an effective answer to Marx:

> Plainly ... the notion that economic insecurity is essential for efficiency and economic advance was ... the common miscalculation of both Marxian and orthodox economists. Marx and his followers were deeply persuaded that capitalism would be crippled by efforts to civilize it. Unemployment compensation, for example, would ruin the operation of the industrial reserve army in regulating wages. In fact, the years of increasing concern for economic security have been ones of unparalleled advance in productivity. [7]

Where Galbraith departs from Keynesian orthodoxy is that he refuses to share its obsession with full employment, which he finds frankly irrational. His argument revolves around the necessity to distinguish between real needs and artificial wants. The USA, argues Galbraith, has almost reached a stage of affluence due to its productive power where it can meet the real needs of all its citizens, so there is no need for further production of necessities. But, in that case, what does one do with the people who, due to advances in technique, are no longer needed to provide essential goods and services? Plainly, given the Keynesian dogma of the desirability of full employment, they must be found jobs producing non-essential goods and services. But why is employing people in order to provide unnecessary work any more rational than freeing them through a guaranteed income to do what they want with their time? Since, in both cases, all one is doing in terms of strict economic logic, is realizing the real wealth of the society in two different ways: either as more consumption or as more leisure. Viewed abstractly, it is the same question as asking whether Plato, furnished with the real wealth of his slave society, would be more rational employing his time in making embroidered nose bags for the donkeys of Athens or employing his time in thinking about life and the universe.

However, Galbraith provides the answer why more consumption was chosen over more leisure. Providing a large number of people with reasonable incomes unrelated to work would require some fairly serious redistribution of wealth. Although it cannot be denied that Keynesianism advocated some redistribution in theory and in practice carried it out through taxation and public spending, its main weapon in alleviating poverty and avoiding recession lay elsewhere, argues Galbraith: in full employment, more production, and economic growth. In this way it could, as Galbraith says in another context, "comfort the afflicted" without "afflicting the comfortable" too much.

So he tells us:

> increased production is an alternative to redistribution. And ..... it has been the great solvent of the tensions associated with inequality .... How much better to concentrate on increasing output, a programme on which both rich and poor can agree, since it benefits both......
>
> It is the increase in output in recent decades, not the redistribution of income, which has brought the great material increase in the well-being of the average man... As a result, the goal of an expanding economy has also become deeply embedded in the conventional wisdom of the American Left. [8]

But this Keynesian choice towards more consumption, warns Galbraith, comes at a price: (1) Full employment policies are bound to be accompanied by inflationary pressures; (2) the accelerated production accompanying full employment is always in danger of not matching consumption, and this danger must be constantly met by public and private debt (government borrowing and spending - especially the "military Keynesianism" of the "industrial-military complex", and also by the easy availability of private credit); (3) it is destructive of the environment in various ways, encouraging "private affluence and public squalor" in Galbraith's phrase.

For all these reasons, as well as the more philosophical reason about how citizens might best choose to *realize* the wealth of their society, thinks Galbraith, the choice of more consumption is not the most rational one.

What is not clear, however, is how Galbraith was able to believe that the redistribution of wealth required for the leisure society he advocated in *The Affluent Society* was realizable under the "Keynesian compromise" of state control of the macro-economy and market control of the micro-economy. It has often been remarked that social democratic governments have the unenviable task of trying to walk a tenuous line between providing their citizens with the kind of generous welfare that gives capitalism an "acceptable face" and at the same time not inhibiting business in its attempts to realize the wealth that makes such welfare possible. Although this balancing act need not in principle be impossible, especially given good will on all sides and a fairly self-contained economy, it is often thought that there is an inevitable tendency for the "Keynesian managers" either to take their "hands off" and give more scope to market forces (which would hardly facilitate redistribution of wealth) or get their "hands on" more fully, culminating in state rather than market determination of all incomes (which would facilitate redistribution of wealth but would no longer be Keynesianism). I suppose it is possible to argue that Keynesianism could indeed achieve something like state-determination of incomes through redistributive tax and income policies but, according to Galbraith, one of the underlying reasons for going the "more production/economic growth" route was precisely to *evade* the awkward task of addressing inequality and redistribution of income. Given that, it seems rather an Achilles Heel in his argument to suggest that this tendency is likely to change or that it will be an easy task to persuade people - especially those with a powerful vested interest in maintaining it - out of it.

Nevertheless, it cannot be denied that *The Affluent Society* is serious economic and social philosophy and that, if realizable, Galbraith's Keynesian leisure society contains many of the features of Marx's

Communist leisure society of "free artistic producers": an ability to distinguish between important and unimportant production of goods and services; a sufficiently advanced industrial state to permit affluence for everyone; redistribution of wealth.

Some of the warning shots that Galbraith sounded about Keynesianism in 1958 did indeed come to fruition: the inflationary pressures, public borrowing, easy credit and an "over-generous money supply". To these, and some other difficulties, I turn now.

IV Inflation, stagflation, globalization, automation

The various factors, their causes, and the links between them that led to difficulties with Keynesianism are so complex and controversial in regard to their relative importance that probably no brief account can be satisfactory. But some account is necessary, so here I shall concentrate on eight main factors: inflation, the OPEC Oil Crises, stagflation, high taxation, the internationalization of capital, increased global competition, automation, and the crisis of the welfare state. In this section, I shall explain what I mean by these terms; in the next section, I shall explore their implications for Keynesianism.

(1) *Inflation* - Why should inflation - a general rise in the level of prices - even matter? The answer seems to be that, given a self-contained economy where incomes always kept up with prices, it would not matter. But, in the real world, even within a self-contained economy, such a neat fit between rises in prices and rises in all incomes is practically impossible. So inflation matters because it is bound to cause instability in the "circular flow of income" between production, consumption, savings and investment, which can then cause social instability and misery. Also, in the real world economies are not self-contained, and so an inflationary economy is bound to be uncompetitive in the world market.

For the purposes of this discussion, I shall distinguish three main types of inflation: (a) "cost-push" inflation, describing price rises due to increasing costs of factors of production such as raw materials or wages;

(b) "demand-pull" inflation, describing price rises due to demand exceeding available supply, with no "slack" in the economy to allow of meeting demand by further (domestic) supply (such as conditions of full employment); (c) the "monetarist" thesis that inflation was basically due to an over-generous money supply (such as easy credit and government borrowing and spending), since the value of money behaved according to the laws of supply and demand like any other commodity: the more of it there was available, the less it was actually worth, so prices would rise accordingly. To be viable, the money supply should always be pegged to long term economic growth to avoid inflation.

(2) *The OPEC Oil Crises* - The trebling or quadrupling of world oil prices by the Oil Producing and Exporting Countries cartel in the 1970s raised the price of the most fundamental raw material of the modern industrial world. The cost-push inflation that resulted unsurprisingly led to such universal price increases for goods and services that world demand slackened and unemployment rose.

(3) *Stagflation* - "Stagflation", and its unlovely twin "slumpflation", can be defined as the coexistence of high inflation and high unemployment. As we have just seen, the OPEC Oil Crises alone are at least partly capable of explaining this phenomenon.

(4) *High Taxation* - Although it now seems generally agreed that Keynesianism largely paid for its "acceptable face of capitalism" - the welfare state - more by economic growth than by serious redistribution of wealth, it cannot be denied that some redistribution did take place, and thus taxes on the wealthy were relatively high. Further, during those periods of its "stop-go" policies when it tried to tackle inflation by fiscal policy, everybody paid higher taxes.

(5) *The Internationalization of Capital* - One aspect of "globalism", it is itself an aspect with several faces. What made it possible was partly new developments in the technologies of transport, communication, and information. What made it feasible for international capital is that it

provided a new means of maintaining or raising profits by cutting costs and/or extending markets and increasing sales. One face of the internationalization of capital was the way that multinational companies resorted to direct foreign investment in order to cut labour costs and/or evade import-barriers to wealthy markets. Another face was the way that freed from restrictions, capital could flow easily between countries and currencies, investing in those which offered the most profit. A further face then became the pressure that it was possible to exert on national governments to adopt policies favourable to global capital. A still further face was a definite shift towards suiting the interests of capital rather than the interests of labour, especially in the developed world. The orthodox view was that precisely such a shift was what was needed, since it was high wages and labour strength that was undermining profitability and the viability of capitalism (one half of Marx's "inner contradiction": high wages leading to a fall in the rate of profit).

(6) *Increased Global Competition* - Another aspect of "globalism", this too has several faces. One is the way that producers in low-cost nations can undercut producers in high-cost ones, in some cases making whole industries more or less redundant and creating major unemployment. Another is the way that multinational corporations can do the same, as when a US multinational moves some or all of its operations to Mexico, causing unemployment among US workers. Sometimes the mere threat of such action is sufficient to exert downward pressure on the costs of labour and suppliers. Another aspect is that global competition pressures companies to cut costs by seeking to make themselves more productive and competitive through automation, reorganization and "downsizing" - so creating further unemployment.

(7) *Automation* - For certain products, the resort to automation is almost inevitable due to pressures to cut costs and to improve product. The resulting "technological unemployment" is usually soaked up by the ever-growing service sector - often low-wage, temporary, and part-time. The macro-economic dangers of this tendency should be obvious (the other half of Marx's "inner contradiction": low wages leading to falling demand

leading to a fall in the rate of profit).

(8) *The Crisis in the Welfare State* - In a sense, some of the crisis in the welfare state is obviously due to the very successes of its noble ambitions: its project of "security from cradle to grave" for all citizens.

In the UK, for instance, it is obvious that the success of the National Health Service is partly what has led to more citizens living a longer and healthier life - with consequent escalating NHS and pensions costs. But these pressures on the costs of the welfare state are greatly increased by pressures from the global economy, forcing governments to prune either the generosity or the universality of their welfare schemes, or both.

V The implications for Keynesianism

It is ironic that during the very period which in theory consisted of the "monetarist reaction" to Keynesianism, President Ronald Reagan in practice launched a binge of Keynesian deficit-spending: tax cuts (for the rich) and increases in defence spending ("military Keynesianism"). Even more, throughout this period, as before, the USA took on the role of "global Keynesian manager" of the world economy, ensuring sufficient aggregate global demand. At times, as Robert Brenner points out, the situation got quite bizarre:

> One witnessed the extraordinary spectacle of Japanese financiers providing the credit needed by the US government to subsidize the continuing growth of Japanese exports. US Keynesianism drove the Japanese boom, but was itself made possible by Japanese loans... It was difficult to determine who was more dependent upon whom - the US Treasury on Japanese lenders or Japanese manufacturers on US borrowers and their demand. What was crystal clear, however, was the degree to which the two leading capitalist economies - and thus the world economy - were dependent upon the historically unprecedented growth of debt in the US and the willingness of the Japanese to help fund it. What perhaps should have been equally obvious was that this process was self-limiting. The subsidy of US demand made possible by Japanese loans was

bound to stimulate the growth of Japanese exports, undermine US production, drive up the US external deficit, and push down the dollar....

When the relative level of US interest rates compared to those abroad began to fall ... the dollar ... plummeted and the yen and mark took off, bringing about a major reversal in competitive advantage ... towards the US. This development was further aided by the effective capping of real wage growth in the US.[9]

Nevertheless, even if Keynes-bashing was sometimes in practice respected more in the breach than the observance, the new movement in economic/political/moral ideas variously known as Thatcherism, Reagonomics, Monetarism, Supply-Side Economics and the New Right was determined to blame Keynesianism for nearly all our economic ills.

Keynesianism was bound to be inflationary, since operating the economy at full employment would produce both demand-pull and cost-push inflation, especially when conjoined with strong unions and the security blanket of a strong welfare state. Further, Keynesian tendencies to be too generous with the money supply were also held by monetarists to be a cause of inflation. Still further, some held there was a form of inflation in the micro-economy which it was held Keynesian macro-economic policy was impotent to arrest: this was the way in which strong unions and large oligopolistic corporations together managed to pass on wage-increases and price-increases to consumers. Finally, Keynesian governments seemed politically reluctant to resort to the required Keynesian remedy: increasing taxes and cutting public spending.

It was presumably a bit unrealistic for the New Right to blame Keynesianism for the OPEC oil crises, but they could try to blame it for stagflation. The argument - elaborately called the "Expectations-Added Phillips Curve" - was that citizens had come to learn that Keynesian policies always tended to produce inflation as the cost of curing unemployment. As a result, citizens had now wised up, so as soon as unemployment showed any sign of a slight fall, they jumped the gun and put in bids for higher wages, since they *expected* inflation soon to rise. Hence the coexistence of relatively high levels of unemployment and inflation. Whether or not Keynesianism was the *cause* of such stagflation - rather than, say, the OPEC oil crisis - the New Right had a stronger case in arguing that Keynesianism had not got the conceptual tools to *deal* with stagflation, since its macro-economic policy consisted in trading off inflation against unemployment, and it lacked the resources to deal with both simultaneously.

Two other Keynesian bad ideas were held to be an over-generous welfare state and the public borrowing and high taxation needed to pay for it. The welfare state plus full employment policies tended to create over-powerful unions who constantly threatened to cripple capital - both state and privately owned capital - with poor performance, strikes, absenteeism, and unrealistic wage demands. Meanwhile, high taxes to support the welfare state also tended to strike at the rich and at business, and to further sap enterprise and wealth-creation.

Not only was this the explanation of the New Right, but also of some of the Far Left, who developed a Marxist-style theory about the inability of Keynesianism to resolve capitalism's difficulties due to the "inner contradictions of Keynesianism". The basic idea is succinctly stated in the following extract:

> the most popular explanation - developed in various forms by Left and Right alike - was that the mechanisms of capitalist growth were undermined by the very success of post-war full employment, which eventually allowed trade unions to take advantage of tight labour markets to force up wages and hold back innovations. The result, it is widely believed, was a cumulative squeeze on profits that broke the springs of investment, and so plunged the world into a prolonged recession. [10]

In a nutshell, then, here we have the one half of Marx's "inner contradiction" (Keynesian policies leading to high wages leading to a fall in the rate of profit). For some on the Far Left, what this situation called for was for even more labour militancy to break the back of capital. For the New Right, the situation called for draconian measures to break the back of labour and restore some equilibrium to capitalism. This would involve dispensing with Keynesian intervention and full employment at unrealistically high wages, giving a freer reign to market forces, subduing labour power, and reforming the welfare state. The needed balance could be tilted back from labour to capital, and profitability restored by a number of interconnected measures: monetarism, supply side economics, changes in union law, and the freeing up of restrictions on global capital.

The monetarist policies, advocated by Milton Friedman and others, did succeed in combating inflation through the effect of high interest rates on consumer demand and business investment. But the inevitable result was recession, so producing the painful trade-off between inflation and unemployment which Keynesian "fine-tuning" had been anxious to avoid. But monetarism did also succeed in effecting what to many was the necessary tilt in the balance of power back towards capital from labour. As J.K. Galbraith observed in 1987:

> monetary policy ... is not socially neutral. It operates against inflation by raising interest rates, which, in turn, inhibit bank lending and resulting deposit - that is, money - creation. High interest rates are wholly agreeable to people and institutions that have money to lend, and these normally have more money than those who have no money to lend or, with many exceptions, those who borrow money. An unduly evident truth... in so favoring the individually and institutionally affluent, a restrictive monetary policy is in sharp contrast with a restrictive fiscal policy, which, relying as it does on increased personal and corporate income taxes, adversely affects the rich." [11]

The same tilting of the balance from labour to capital was also achieved by what came to be known as "supply-side economics" through a system of tax cuts that in practice benefited the rich. One leading idea was as counter-intuitive as Keynes's idea that you could spend your way out of a recession, since supply-side economics held that *by cutting taxes governments could increase their overall tax yield.* The underlying logic here was the same as that of a business which believes that, by lowering prices, it will increase its profits because it will sell more.

Fundamentally, this was yet more Keynes-bashing, since it was held that Keynesian demand-management was stifling the supply-side of the economy, inhibiting private enterprise, investment, and economic growth, not the least through high taxation. Robert Heilbroner and Lester Thurow explain it more fully:

> As the words indicate, supply-side economics is more concerned with supply - production - than with demand or buying... What is crucial is their belief that the volume of private demand, once the public sector has been pulled back, will be large enough to provide high employment and vigorous growth. 'Produce the goods', they say, 'and the purchasing power to buy them will be created in the act of production itself'.
>
> And will there be *enough* production, the great worry of the demand-siders? Yes, say the supply-side economists, provided that the incentive to produce is given its due. The supply-side image of the economy is that of a great spring, held down by the weight of high marginal taxes and excessive [public] spending. Take away the taxes that discourage risk-taking and expansion, roll back the government spending that absorbs labour and resources that ought to be available to the private sector, and the inherent dynamism in the spring will manifest itself. [12]

It was the great wave of new investment by the private sector that was supposed to be unleashed by such tax cuts that was the rationale behind supply-side philosophy, since it was this that was supposed to provide both full employment and a higher overall tax yield due to the newly invigorated economy. But all this was only partly forthcoming:

> One of the rosy predictions made in the days when the supply-side slogan was first coined was that cutting taxes would unleash such a mighty wave of investment that GNP would rise enough to generate *more* tax revenues, despite the lower tax rates. That hope proved to be a chimera - the cut in taxes did help GNP grow, but the growth was nowhere near enough to increase the government's revenue, adjusted for inflation...
>
> Another thing we know is that cutting taxes and expenditures can create problems as well as alleviate them ... An increase in well-being at the top was... offset by an increase in ill-being at the bottom. As part of its income distribution problem, the 1980s produced a rise in poverty - the first such rise in two generations. [13]

But, of course, just such a redistribution of wealth - and power - from labour to capital, it was held, was what was needed in order to restore the viability of capitalism

To many commentators perhaps the most significant way of restoring the necessary equilibrium between capital and labour power, and perhaps the most formidable objection to Keynesianism, lies in the phenomenon of the freeing up of controls on capital to seek its advantage at the expense of labour on a global scale. Keynesian demand-management crucially depended on the ability to exert control over the whole economy at a *national* level; the growing *internationalization* of capital effectively weakened its power to do so. John Gray makes the point well in the following extract:

> Economic globalization removes, or weakens, the policy levers whereby social democratic governments sought to bring about social solidarity and egalitarian redistribution. Full employment cannot be promoted by aggressive deficit financing because that is now being interdicted by global bond markets (as the Swedish social democrats discovered). Using the tax system to promote goals of income and wealth redistribution is severely constrained by unprecedented international mobility of capital and people. Globalization weakens or undermines the bargaining power of organised labour. Public financing of the welfare state is constrained by dependency on global capital markets, which limit to a narrow range national governments' leverage over interest rates and exchange rates. The magnitudes of these effects... on national economies and governments remain controversial. What is less controversial is the conviction that they will become ever more significant in future. [14]

Andre Gorz is still more explicit:

> When economic growth was halted....the technocratic state which was the indispensable broker of that [Keynesian] compromise lost its legitimacy in the eyes of the bourgeoisie. It could only retain its powers of regulation and arbitration by restraining the play of the market more than it had previously done and by substituting an administered capitalism, ever closer to state capitalism, for the free-market variety. Which meant that the state would have to engage in a head-on clash with the bourgeoisie.
>
> The rest is history...... The regulatory power of the nation state had, in the

event, been overcome from another direction, namely by the internationalization of capital and, most importantly, by the development of a financial market on a world scale. To maintain their powers of economic intervention, the national tecnocracies would have had to confront not just their own national bourgeoisies, but the financial bourgeoisies and the central banks of all the industrialized capitalist nations. The opening up of national economies to the world market and the exacerbation of international competition thus became a sovereign weapon for the national bourgeoisies against a state interventionism operating only on the scale of a single country ...

The market - or rather the opening up of national economies to a world market beyond the regulatory power of nation states - thus recovered its original *political* function, which was to prevent the political control of the economy... No one, neither governments nor industrialists, nor finance capital could be held responsible for the constraints imposed by competition on the world market ...

This explains the crisis, retreat and malaise of the European Left. Once one allows the market to impose 'competitiveness' as the prime and irresistible imperative, then...'society has to be managed as an auxiliary of the market'. The welfare state thus has to be dismantled and the economy 'deregulated', liberal capitalist ideology tends to become hegemonic and the Left... governs in the name of efficiency and technocratic coherence. It embodies the art of mediation between 'balance of payments pressures' on the one hand and the interests of the wage-earning strata on the other. In short, it is Left or socialist only in name - a name which it merely discredits. [15]

VI The implications for Marxism

The orthodox analysis of the trials and tribulations that affected the global economy in the 1970s was that Keynesian full employment policies led to powerful organized labour, higher wages, and a falling rate of profit for capital. Both Right and Left took this as a sign that Keynesianism had been discredited in its attempts to allow a stable and acceptable face of capitalism through its "fine-tuning" attempts and its "welfare economics". On this much they agreed. But whereas the Right assumed that the failure of Keynesian intervention triumphantly proved the virtues of deregulation, *laissez-faire*, and Adam Smith's "benign invisible hand" of equilibrium established through market forces, the Left assumed that the failure of the "Keynesian compromise" triumphantly proved the virtues of Marx's original analysis. For had not Marx said:

> crises are precisely always preceded by a period in which wages rise generally and the working class actually get a larger share ... It seems, then, that capitalist production comprises certain conditions which are independent of good or bad will and permit the working class to enjoy that relative prosperity only momentarily, and at that always as a harbinger of a coming crisis. [16]

On this analysis, then, tilting the balance back from labour to capital will only restore stability at the price of tending to further instability - New Right policies leading to unemployment, underemployment and low wages leading to underconsumption leading to a falling rate of profit.

As Robert Brenner says:

> Since the victories of Reaganism-Thatcherism at the end of the 1970s, capital has greatly deepened its domination, especially in the US. Wage growth has been effectively repressed. Fiscal austerity, combined with tight credit, has brought universal deflation. The rich have benefited from several rounds of tax reduction. Industry after industry has been deregulated to weaken unions which had benefited from their formerly administered prices. The global flow of capital has been progressively unfettered so that multinational corporations and banks can better scour the world to find the most profitable location for their activities. Finance has been unshackled, to create ever more baroque means to squeeze more money from money. The brutal stabilization policies of the World Bank and the IMF have been accepted as gospel. What is more, the Statist regimes of the former Soviet Union and Eastern Europe have collapsed, and China has taken the capitalist road. Yet, despite all this, things are not going smoothly for capitalism. [17]

For Brenner, the dangers of the underconsumption tendencies of New Right policies of holding down wages are further exacerbated - and even *caused* by - what he sees as another, and in his eyes deeper, explanation of the crisis that affected global capitalism in the 1970s - overproduction tendencies following from overcapacity in the world economy leading to overcompetition and a falling rate of profit.

Brenner's analysis focuses on other features of Marx's original analyses: the way that a falling rate of profit may be precipitated by a combination of the organic composition of capital, competition, and the "anarchy of capitalist production":

> For its most intelligent champions, of course, competition is the central virtue of capitalism as an economic system - the discipline that makes it supremely innovative, giving it easy victory over the command economies in the Cold War. Brenner takes the system at its word, and shows how its strongest claim to productivity also fatally brings on loss of momentum and recurrent crisis. Successful competition in manufacturing typically requires the sinking of large amounts of investment in complexes of fixed capital. These, however, will tend to become outdated by technologically newer complexes, initially erected in spaces beyond immediate reprisal by the original enterprises. The competitive pressure of the later arrivals then inevitably depresses the rate of return on the older enterprises. But these cannot immediately liquidate the capital sunk in fixed plant, with a normal life-span still to run, to exit into other lines of production. Instead, their rational response will be to lower their margins to meet the challenge from more efficient newcomers. The result is a pattern of over-competition forcing down the rate of profit throughout the branch concerned. Once such competition becomes generalized, opportunities for profit contract, investment declines, and at some stage a sharp downturn becomes inevitable - which will last until sufficient obsolete capital has been flushed out of the system to re-start the mechanism of accumulation at full tilt again. [18]

One cannot but admire the way in which Brenner's painstaking analysis has managed to think beyond the orthodox account and to conclude that the ills of global capitalism are due rather to a "horizontal" competition between capitals rather than a "vertical" struggle between capital and labour (and that the "vertical" struggle between capital and labour in countries such as the USA and the UK in the Reagan/Thatcher years was prompted by a deeper "horizontal" struggle between the rival capitalisms of the US, the UK, Japan, Germany, and the "Asian Tiger" economies). One must also admire the way that he succeeds in showing how the ideas of that "defunct economist" Marx are still relevant. As when Brenner says:

> My point of departure is ... simultaneously that capitalism tends to develop the productive forces to an unprecedented degree, and that it tends to do so in a destructive, because *unplanned and competitive manner*.......
>
> We therefore need a theory of a malign invisible hand to go along with Adam Smith's benign one - a theory which can encompass a self-generating *series of steps* resulting from individual (and collective) profit maximizing which leads not towards adjustment, but rather away from it. [19]

That being said, one can argue that a number of crucial questions are still being begged. These questions fall basically into three sorts: (1) Planning versus Market; (2) "Utopian" and "Scientific" Socialism; (3) Environmental Limits and Constraints. It is to these I turn now.

(1) *Planning versus Market* - Marxist diagnoses of the ills of the capitalist economy habitually refer to "planning" as a crucial part of the necessary cure in the prevention of economic cycles of boom and bust, crisis and instability. But, whether we are talking about national, regional or global planning there are several well-known problems to be addressed.

Firstly, there is the vagueness, utopianism, and "If I ruled the world" flavour about so many Marxist recommendations of cures through "planning".

Secondly, there is the problem that where regional planning is the paradigm, how are the regions to be related? Are we speaking here of self-sufficiency, market relations, global coordinating plans, or what?

Thirdly, there are a number of technical criticisms concerning the difficulties of replacing markets with planning. For instance, there is the criticism of Ludwig von Mises that any system which lacks markets to cost factors in terms of supply and demand is bound to be irrational, and, as a result, to be wasteful, inefficient, haphazard, prone to shortages and gluts and needlessly extravagant production costs. The argument here is that effective planning cannot even *in principle* replace the market. Then there are the criticisms of F. von Hayek and others that *in practice* the logistics of planning would be too complex to be anything but inferior to production, distribution, and exchange through the market. Also, there are the well-known arguments concerning the problem of replacing the incentive provided by the profit and money motive of the market, held to be so crucial to enterprise and innovation. Taken together, all these criticisms, especially in the hands of the New Right, were used against all forms of socialist economics in tandem with their criticisms of Keynesian demand management and intervention. What they all fundamentally argue, of course, is that if Marx decried capitalism as irrational, wasteful, and inefficient, then any conceivable socialist alternative must be even more so.

Fourthly, there is a set of problems concerning planning that touch on its political and moral implications. All involve the danger of tyranny. The basic argument is that socialist society may well be more oppressive than capitalist society. For instance, what discipline is supposed to replace the "discipline of the market"? For it is foolish to imagine that any complex economic system can work without discipline to ensure efficiency, innovation, and smooth functioning, however well-intentioned its participants might be. There are always those who, looking at the lessons of Soviet history, worry with some reason that execution, prisons, labour camps, and starvation can be the disciplinary "stick" which replaces the "tyranny of the market", while corruption, cronyism, and the favours of political office can be the "carrot" replacing the "almighty dollar". More mildly, we should remember that twentieth century Soviet workers were forbidden to strike, just as were nineteenth American workers, although for different reasons: not because this would be a monopoly of labour that might upset capital's profits, but because it was a logical impossibility: the workers owned the means of production, and so would only be striking against themselves! Another dimension of possible tyranny concerns the ancient political issue of "separation of powers". Liberals have always argued that one of the major virtues of the private property system of capitalism is that it guards against the potential tyranny that can happen when political and economic powers are fused, rather than separated. Although this liberal argument cut little ice with Marx, on the grounds that he believed that such separation of powers was more apparent than real (since government would always protect the interests of capital), it is not a worthless argument. As Michael Barratt Brown observes:

> Those who used to argue that this separation is superfluous, once overwhelming power is in the hands of the elected representatives of working people, have had to think again in the light of what we now know of the victims of the Soviet trials of the 1930s, of Stalin's Gulag ... and of Chinese dissidents ...
>
> The fact is that the more powers of government planning in the economy we have to allow for, the more necessary it is that power should not be concentrated - even in the hands of the good and the just, lest they be tempted to abuse it - and should be accountable to the people. [20]

Finally, it is worth observing that the closest the global economy has come to being "planned" is probably the way that the USA undertook to be the Keynesian-style global manager of aggregate demand (see Note 9). The fact that this happened, as well as the fact that it was not entirely successful, should tell us something about both the potential and the difficulty of "planning the economy", especially on a global scale.

(2) *"Utopian" and "Scientific" Socialism* - It is all very well to dream about some form or other of "planning", but from the perspective of Marxist "scientific socialism", this can only be the most vapid form of "utopian socialism", unless one can clearly indicate which real historical forces are likely to effect such a change. For perhaps the chief defining difference for Marx between utopian and scientific socialism is that the scientific socialist, like Marx himself, thinks he has detected historical forces bubbling under that merely need a bit of a push; whereas the utopian socialist is a dreamer playing at "If I ruled the world" in a historical vacuum.

Candidates for the architects of such "planning" have been various. For Marx himself writing in the context of nineteenth century capitalism, it was of course the proletariat of industrialized Europe, the ever-growing mass of impoverished, disaffected workers who nevertheless constituted an increasingly united, educated force, quite capable of taking the management of a planned economy into their own hands. For Joseph

Schumpeter, writing in the 1940s after the New Deal in the USA and at the inception of the British welfare state, the required revolutionary force was the increasingly comfortable, rather than impoverished, recipients of bureaucratic corporate capitalism and the welfare state - precipitating a socialist rather than a capitalist ethos. For Herbert Marcuse, writing in the turbulent affluence of 1960s America, it was a coalition of forces at the top and the bottom of the social scale: young middle class radicals and drop-outs disaffected with the "American Dream" in tandem with the oppressed minorities whom the Dream had largely passed by (what we should now probably call the "underclass" and what Marx called the *Lumpenproletariat*).

This question, then, of whether there are any such "historical revolutionary forces" at the end of the twentieth century, of the kind that Marx thought he detected at the end of the nineteenth, needs to be addressed.

(3) *Environmental Limits and Constraints* - There exists a blanket environmentalist criticism of all forms of growth economics to the effect that the dream of universal prosperity through unlimited growth is no longer feasible.

Applied to Marxist ideas, it is easy to see why this criticism has some force. It is a central part of Marx's idea of the good society that (a) it will be a society where no one suffers from scarcity; (b) that the removal of scarcity will be made possible by the enormous "boosting of productive forces" previously stifled by capitalist modes of distribution through effective financial demand; and (c) that in a society where everyone has more than enough of everything, there will be no more war or conflict, since war and conflict are essentially about struggle for scarce resources leading to class society.

Not only is this vision subject to the quite reasonable criticism that it is a naive and oversimplified view of human nature and an absurdly reductive account of the causes of war and conflict, but it is also subject to the equally reasonable criticism that it is environmental insanity. No matter how many "high-tech fixes" of environmental problems one dreams of, and no matter how much relatively non-polluting service sectors replace manufacturing sectors, the dream of universal abundance in an overloaded planet is an unworkable equation.

It seems to me that Marxists can only hope to answer these two criticisms in the following way: (a) they can insist, with equal reasonableness, that struggles over scarce resources are still the *major* cause of war and conflict, even if not the *sole* cause; (b) they can argue that the undeniable Marxist emphasis on the removal of scarcity is balanced by the equally undeniable emphasis on the need to distinguish between real and superfluous needs - the kind of criticism that J.K. Galbraith levelled at the pointlessness of much production in 1950s America.

How do environmentalist criticisms apply to contemporary global capitalism? Here, it seems, the dream is something as follows: the best way to ensure global prosperity is through global free trade; economic growth may gradually allow Africans to enjoy the standards of living that Europeans enjoy now; but in order for Africans to grow economically, they must be able to rely on the wealthy developed world as a market. Hence the economic growth of the one depends on the economic growth of the other. Africa needs to sell bananas, trainers, and tourism to Europe; Europe needs to be wealthy enough to buy them.

Galbraith's analysis in *The Affluent Society* seems equally relevant here. For is not this free market dream of global prosperity essentially repeating his arguments about 1950s America: economic growth is the preferred route because it helps both rich and poor without needing to seriously address questions of inequality and redistribution of wealth? It is a way of "comforting the afflicted" without "afflicting the comfortable". Just as the car workers in Galbraith's USA needed the wealthy to keep buying more Cadillacs to keep them in a job, so the "wretched of the earth" need designers in Paris to be wealthy enough to be tourists in Africa and Asia. Any talk about real and apparent needs could only be unhelpful here, since, even if prompted by environmental concerns, it would damage the dream of painless prosperity through economic growth.

All these questions and doubts, then, remain. But what can be concluded is that Marx's basic ideas about overproduction, underconsumption and crises are still relevant to contemporary global capitalism.

Hence - Marx's good idea.

Notes

1. Karl Marx (Capital III, 15:1), *Marx on Economics*, pp. 171-172.
2. K. Marx (Capital III, 30), Ibid., pp. 173-174.
3. J.K. Galbraith, *The Affluent Society*, Penguin, 1971, pp. 82-83.
4. K. Marx (Capital II, 20:4), *Marx on Economics*, p. 174.
5. Michael Barratt Brown, *Models in Political Economy*, pp. 59-60.
6. George Dalton, *Economic Systems and Society*, Penguin, 1983, p. 104.
7. J.K. Galbraith, *The Affluent Society*, pp. 118-119.
8. J.K. Galbraith, Ibid., pp. 104-105.
9. Robert Brenner, *The Economics of Global Turbulence*, New Left Review, 1998, pp. 183-184.
10. R. Brenner, Ibid., p. iii, Editorial Introduction.
11. J.K. Galbraith, *A History of Economics*, Penguin, 1991, p. 273.
12. Robert Heilbroner and Lester Thurow, *Economics Explained*, Simon & Schuster, 1994, p. 126.
13. R. Heilbroner and L. Thurow, Ibid., pp. 126-127.
14. John Gray, *After Social Democracy*, Demos, 1996, p. 32.
15. Andre Gorz, *Critique of Economic Reason*, pp. 188-189.
16. K. Marx (Capital II, 20:4), *Marx on Economics*, p. 174.
17. R. Brenner, *The Economics of Global Turbulence*, p. 235.
18. R. Brenner, Ibid., p. iii-iv, Editorial Introduction.
19. R. Brenner, Ibid., p. 23.
20. M. Barratt Brown, *Models in Political Economy*, p. 251.

3 Schumpeter and Socialism: Big is Beautiful

Introduction

As an economist and social philosopher, Joseph Schumpeter was certainly odd. One of the oddest things about him was his attitude to Marxism, stated most fully in his 1943 classic, *Capitalism, Socialism and Democracy*. There, he treats the reader to numerous swipes at the "Marxist faithful", who are invariably portrayed as ignorant of both economic theory and economic realities, and who comfort themselves by dutifully reciting the sacred texts of the great prophet Marx to quell any external criticisms or self-doubts. Nor is the prophet himself spared by Schumpeter: most of Marx's central economic ideas are found wanting.

The odd thing is that, in spite of all this, Schumpeter ends up confirming the most important item on the Marxist agenda: capitalism will destroy itself from within and (most probably) its successor will be socialism. The heretical twist which Schumpeter gives to this argument is to claim that capitalism will not fail because of its economic deficiencies ("inner contradictions") but because of its very successes in delivering the goods ("removing scarcity", "promoting human welfare").

What principally concerns Schumpeter is the economic organization of socialism. So a crucial part of *Capitalism, Socialism and Democracy* is concerned with arguing the following three theses: central planning is the most suitable candidate for socialist economic organization; it can withstand all criticisms about its rationality and workability as an economic system; it is in a number of important ways a better economic system than capitalism (even if no cast-iron guarantees can be given to the "Marxist faithful" that it will produce heaven on earth or a "better human clay").

With the hindsight of history, must we not say that all of this must now sound distinctly quaint? And that the shade of Schumpeter (who died in 1950) - if confronted by such facts as the abysmal collapse of the Soviet central planning experiment, the "crisis of Keynesianism", the celebratory return to the market of Thatcherism and Reagonomics, and the contemporary dominance, even if not trouble-free, of global capitalism - would be forced to say: "Well, yes, I think I got it a bit wrong. 'Market socialism' - perhaps. Blairite 'Third Ways' between market and state, New Right and Old Labour - possibly. But central planning - no!"?

Perhaps he would concede this. But there would be no necessity about him doing so, and nor do I think he would have been particularly surprised at the way things have turned out. Schumpeter, just as much as the "Marxist faithful", held to the view that the USSR could not be regarded as a Marxist socialist society: it was too "unripe" - and so too perhaps was the rest of the world. Similarly, he is at one with the "Marxist faithful" in being dubious about any long-term viability for the "Keynesian compromise", of "welfare economics", of the reformist "halfway house" of state management of the macro-economy and market management of the micro-economy. He seems to have believed that, for effective economic functioning, Keynesianism would either have to get its "hands more fully on" (i.e., transmute into central planning) or else have to take its "hands off" (i.e. transmute back into the kind of championing of market forces, privatization, and "rolling back of the state" which actually happened).

What makes Schumpeter so challenging today, such a "Socratic gadfly", is the uncompromising nature of his position: not only is capitalism probably on the way out, but the most logical form of replacement is probably central planning. If a thinker of his acuteness could seriously believe this, does it not make us at least wonder if the reason why the idea of central planning seems hardly on anyone's agenda anymore (and why socialism in general, and Marxism in particular, are in such bad odour) may be more due to ideology and fashion than sound argument and unstoppable realities?

In what follows, I divide the discussion into three parts: (1) Schumpeter's criticisms of Marx; (2) the viability of central planning; (3) the superiority of the "socialist blueprint".

I Schumpeter's criticisms of Marx

(1) *Surplus Value and the Labour Theory of Value* - Building on Locke, Smith, and Ricardo, Marx argues that human labour is the source of economic value. This enables him to arrive at his famous theory of surplus value ("exploitation"). What the capitalist hirer pays the worker (exchange-value) is less than the work (use-value) which he extracts from him or her. Hence capitalist profits accrue from this "surplus value". Now, the capitalist sensibly - and spurred by competition - realizes that he can get bigger profits from his workers by making them more productive through the use of machinery. Thus we get the "organic composition of capital" - defined as the relation between men (waged labourers, "variable capital" or "v") and machines (or "constant capital" or "c"). But now comes the distressing result. As the organic composition of capital tilts towards machines (c) at the expense of men (v), the rate of profit must fall. Why? Because the base which is the sole source of surplus value, and hence profit - human workers, living labour, v - has dwindled, even though productivity has increased, as industry becomes more capital-intensive and less labour-intensive. This *must* be so, as a matter of logic, since Marx has deduced labour as the real source of value and surplus value as the real source of profit.

Common sense will perhaps want to say that it is the machines, rather than their operators, which have created the extra value through increased productivity (or at least a combination of the two). But, given the labour theory of value which Marx espouses, it is not possible to say this. A rather fanciful thought-experiment illustrates the weirdness of this. Suppose, as technology proceeds apace, a fully automated factory where machines do all the work, owned by a single capitalist with a single employee - a security guard. It follows from the Marxist analysis that all the profits that the capitalist owner is getting out of his automated factory must in the final analysis stem from the surplus value/exploitation of the security guard, since he is the only living labour (v) left around.

Schumpeter believes we can cut through this strange logic by finding a more satisfactory analytic apparatus which can account for value and profit in terms of *all* the factors of production - land, capital, labour - rather than just labour. He believes that the marginal utility theory of value can do just this, and so avoid some counter-intuitive absurdities. But if we replace the labour theory of value, then Marx's whole argument about surplus value, the organic composition of capital, and the inevitability of a falling rate of profit which will ultimately destroy capitalism falls to the ground:

> The aggregate rate of profit on total industrial capital need not fall in the long run, either for the Marxian reason that the constant capital increases relatively to the variable capital or for any other. [1]

Schumpeter does, however, proceed to qualify this argument in favour of Marx:

> It is sufficient that ... the profit of every individual plant is incessantly being threatened by actual or potential competition from new commodities or methods of production which sooner or later will turn it into a loss. So we get the driving force required and even an analogon to Marx's proposition that constant capital does not produce surplus value - for no individual assemblage of capital goods remains a source of surplus gains forever - without having to rely on those parts of his argument which are of doubtful validity. [2]

In other words (as Schumpeter so often declares), Marx was right, but for the wrong reasons.

(2) *Overproduction/Underconsumption* - It is probably fair to say that one of the "inner contradictions" of capitalism for Marx is its simultaneous need for high employment and high unemployment. Capitalism needs high employment for the (to Schumpeter, dubious) reason that living labour is the source of surplus value, hence profits; also for the more mundane and plausible reason that employed people generally have more money than unemployed people and so can function as consumers, consuming the goods that capitalism produces for sale. Because, obviously, for capitalism to function well, mass consumption (or sales) must equal mass production. At the same time, capitalism requires a high amount of unemployment - an "industrial reserve army" - to drive down wages, to be laid off in bad times

and to be pulled in to work in good times.

Now, it is clearly part of Marx's argument that "technological unemployment" is a pervasive feature of modern capitalism. As technology gets more sophisticated, as industry and commerce get more "rationalized" and "mechanized", more and more people are thrown out of work. Although this has the advantage of driving down wage rates, it has the disadvantage of producing "less effective financial demand" - that is, of producing a situation where not enough people have enough money to consume the full product which capitalists need to sell at an advantageous price if they are not to make a loss.

Hence we get overproduction/underconsumption, and perhaps the prime instance of what for Marx was the central "inner contradiction" of capitalism: the "mode of exchange" ("Have you got the money to pay for it?") holds back the full potential of the "forces of production" because capitalist production is geared only to meeting human need that is backed up by financial demand. If you haven't got the work, and hence the money, then from a strict capitalist viewpoint, you must, in Adolf Hitler's classic phrase, be "a useless eater", a social cost rather than a social benefit.

There are those (like Jeremy Rifkin in *The End of Work*) who argue that Marx's prophetic musings on "technological unemployment" are what help to make him still relevant today, and that he would surely say "I told you so" if confronted by the kind of technological unemployment produced, for instance, by the "micro-chip revolution" in industry and commerce.

By comparison, Schumpeter is both more conventional and more optimistic; but also thought-provoking. Schumpeter is glad to admit that the "creative destruction" of capitalism *does* produce unemployment, bankruptcy, and wholesale redundancy of technologies and firms that fail to adapt. The automobile replaces the horse and buggy; the word-processor replaces the typewriter. But, in spite of the disruption, such "creative destruction" also opens up new technological possibilities, new demand, new markets, new avenues for investment, new enterprise and new employment:

> Technological possibilities are an uncharted sea ... there is no reason to expect a slackening of the rate of output through exhaustion of technological possibilities. [3]

The promise held out by the chemical industry alone is much greater than it was possible to anticipate in, say, 1880. [4]

Presumably, Schumpeter would enlist such recent developments as gene-technology in agriculture and medicine to support his thesis. And perhaps also, he might try to turn a standard environmentalist criticism of capitalism (and of growth economics generally) on its head by arguing that the next great revolution in the "creative destruction" of capitalism will consist - if it is not already doing so - in making a profit out of meeting the pressing demands for new "environmental technology" (non-polluting fuels, solutions to global warming, investment in forests to absorb emissions from pollution, etc.).

At all events, at this point in his argument, Schumpeter clearly adopts the non-Marxist position that there is no obvious economic reason why the "capitalist engine" should fail:

We may put some trust in the ability of the capitalist engine to find or create ever new opportunities since it is geared to that very purpose. [5]

He also bolsters his argument by suggesting that the past performance of capitalism, if continued, could render what unemployment remains acceptable without a transition to socialism:

I hold that the real tragedy is not unemployment *per se*, but unemployment plus the impossibility of providing adequately for the unemployed *without impairing the conditions of further economic growth*: for obviously the suffering and degradation - the destruction of human values - which we associate with unemployment, though not the waste of productive resources, would be largely eliminated and unemployment would lose practically all its terror if the private life of the unemployed were not seriously affected by their unemployment. The indictment stands that in the past - say, roughly to the end of the nineteenth century - the capitalist order was not only unwilling but also quite incapable of guaranteeing this. But since it will be able to do so if it keeps up its past performance for another half century this indictment would in that case enter the limbo filled by the sorry specters of child labor and sixteen-hour working days and five persons living in one room which it is quite proper to emphasize when talking about the past social costs of capitalist achievement but which are not necessarily relevant to the balance of alternatives in the future. Our own time is somewhere between the disabilities of earlier stages in capitalist evolution and the abilities of the system in full maturity. In this country at least, the better part of the task could even now be accomplished without undue strain on the system. [6]

(3) *Immiseration of the Proleteriat* - Schumpeter's scepticism about the labour theory of value and his belief that capitalism may continue to find new opportunities for investment and employment naturally leads him to be sceptical also of Marx's doctrine of the "immiseration of the proleteriat", since it is a logically connected thesis. The increasing misery and poverty of the working class is deduced in the Marxist system from the desperate attempts of competing capitalists to escape from the "inner contradictions" of capitalism. It may take the forms of trying to squeeze out more productivity per worker ("sweated labour" and/or improved technology) or of the attendant miseries of unemployment and underemployment (insecure, temporary, low-paid work).

Schumpeter comments:

Marx undoubtedly held that in the course of capitalist evolution real wage rates and the standard of life of the masses would fall in the better paid, and fail to improve in the worst-paid strata and that this would come about not through any accidental or environmental circumstances but by virtue of the very logic of the capitalist process. As a prediction, this was of course singularly infelicitous... Then attempts were made to read into it a different meaning, that is to say, to make it refer not to rates of real wages or to the absolute share that goes to the working class but to the relative share of labour incomes in total national income. Though some passages in Marx will in fact bear this interpretation, this clearly violates the meaning of most. Moreover, little would be gained by accepting this interpretation, because Marx's main conclusions presuppose that the *absolute* per capita share of labour should fall or, at the very least, not

> increase: if he had really been thinking of the relative share that would only add to Marxian troubles. Finally the proposition itself would still be wrong. For the relative share of wages and salaries in total income varies but little from year to year and is remarkably consistent over time - it certainly does not reveal any tendency to fall. [7]

For Schumpeter, both the absolute and relative interpretations of "immiseration" are false: it is not the case that the poor of 1950 are poorer in absolute terms than the poor of 1900; nor is it the case that, although living standards for *all* are rising, the poor of 1950 are relatively worse off in comparison to the rich than they were in 1900.

Schumpeter could be questioned on this. There are those, like Immanuel Wallerstein, who argue that, if we think in terms of global capitalist operations, the poor in many parts of the Third World *are* getting *absolutely* poorer. (The so-called "exploitation thesis" of Third World development). And there are those who point out that, in *relative* terms, the policies of recent supply-side economics *have* resulted in a redistribution of wealth from poor to rich, so that, even if general living standards have risen, the poor in 1990 in the U.K. may well be relatively poorer than in 1950.

But even if Schumpeter granted this, he could still maintain that there was nothing inherently necessary about it, as the "Marxist faithful" would have us believe. For any necessity about it could only spring from the basic Marxist concepts (surplus value, organic composition of capital, falling rate of profit) which Schumpeter is so sceptical about. So the main thrust of Schumpeter's argument is that, given an endless horizon of technological, investment and employment opportunities, the "'capitalist engine" almost cannot help but improve the lot of everyone, since its mass production techniques are geared to mass consumption. So he tells us:

> I have stated ... that, broadly speaking, relative shares in national income have remained substantially constant over the last hundred years. This, however, is true only if we measure them in money. Measured in real terms, relative shares have substantially changed in favor of the lower income groups. This follows from the fact that the capitalist engine is first and last an engine of mass production which unavoidably means also production for the masses.... .

> It is the cheap cloth, the cheap cotton and rayon fabric, boots, motor cars and so on that are the typical achievements of capitalist production, and not as a rule improvements that would mean much to the rich man. Queen Elizabeth owned silk stockings. The capitalist achievement does not typically consist in providing more silk stockings for queens but in bringing them within the reach of factory girls in return for steadily decreasing amounts of effort. [8]

(4) *Concentration of Capital and Monopoly* - So far we have seen Schumpeter being highly critical of Marx. But we are now about to see him move, in however maverick a fashion, towards the Marxist camp. He has high praise for Marx's prophetic insights about the concentration of capital and monopoly. Schumpeter says:

> his Theory of Concentration, that is, his treatment of the tendency of the capitalist process to increase the size both of industrial plants and of units of control. All he has to offer in explanation, when stripped of his imagery, boils down to the unexciting statements that 'the battle of competition is fought by cheapening commodities' which 'depends, *caeteris paribus*, on the productivenuss of labor'; that this again depends on the scale of production; and that 'the larger capital beats the smaller'. This is much like what the current textbook says on the matter, and is not very deep or admirable in itself....
>
> Yet the admiration so many economists outside the fold profess to feel for this theory is not unjustified. For one thing, to predict the advent of big business was, considering the conditions of Marx's day, an achievement in itself. But he did more than that. He neatly hitched concentration to the process of accumulation or rather he visualized the former as part of the latter, and not only as part of its factual pattern but also of its logic. He perceived some of the consequences correctly - for instance that 'the increasing bulk of individual masses of capital becomes the material basis of an uninterrupted revolution in the mode of production itself'. [9]

If "growing big" (concentrating capital) is one way of staying ahead in the "creative destruction" of capitalist competition, then another - and related - way is to control the effects of adverse competition on oneself by being big enough to dominate markets, to restrict competition and inflate profits, either singly or in concert with other "big boys", through such processes as price-fixing and restricting supply. Hence we get a range of associated phenomena: monopoly, oligopoly, trusts and cartels. Perhaps the most succinct exposition of the role of such phenomena in Marxism is provided by Engels. Engels says:

> Many of these means of production and distribution are, from the outset, so colossal, that, like the railroads, they exclude all other forms of capitalistic exploitation. At a further stage of evolution this form also becomes insufficient. The producers on a large scale in a particular branch of industry in a particular country unite in a 'Trust', a union for the purpose of regulating production. They determine the total amount to be produced, parcel it out among themselves, and thus enforce the selling price fixed beforehand. But trusts of this kind, as soon as business becomes bad, are generally liable to break up, and, on this very account, compel a yet greater concentration of association. The whole of the particular industry is turned into one gigantic joint-stock company; internal competition gives place to the internal monopoly of this one company. This has happened in 1890 with the English *alkali* production, which is now, after the fusion of 48 large works, in the hands of one company, conducted upon a single plan ... ..
>
> In the trusts, freedom of competition changes into its very opposite - into monopoly; and the production without any definite plan of capitalistic society capitulates to the production upon a definite plan of the invading socialistic society. Certainly this is so far still to the benefit and advantage of the capitalists. But in this case the exploitation is so palpable that it must break down. No nation will put up with production conducted by trusts, with so barefaced an exploitation of the community by a small band of dividend-mongers.
>
> In any case, with trusts or without, the official representative of capitalist society - the State - will ultimately have to undertake the direction of production. This necessity for conversion into State-property is felt first in the great institutions for intercourse and communication - the post-office, the telegraphs, the railways. [10]

Contained in this passage from Engels are many of the key features also contained in Schumpeter's maverick brand of Marxism. The central contention is the following: the *ethos and practice of socialism is insidiously infecting the ethos and practice of capitalism*: this is what is secretly contained in the drift towards planning, the concentration of big business into vast, complex bureaucracies, the replacement of "hands on" capitalist owners with salaried managers and executives, and the tendency towards monopolistic practices.

I should mention two caveats, however. Engels shares with conventional free market economists a loathing of trusts and monopoly - both agree that this is "barefaced ... exploitation of the community". Schumpeter characteristically gives the argument two unexpected twists. First, he argues that, in however cockeyed a fashion, the kind of collaboration shown by managers of different enterprises in a cartel in fixing production and distribution is

> a most important step toward socialism [11]

exactly the kind of thing which socialist managers will need to do to coordinate their activities. Second, he argues for the often benign effects of some of the monopolistic practices of big business, even within a capitalist context. The kind of breathing space allowed by the protective walls of short-term price-fixing by big business, he argues, often is the means to a far more significant long-term reduction in prices due to the new research and development, new technology and greater productivity allowed by those very protective walls. In fact, he argues that such imperfect competition is probably a better way to get maximum productivity out of the "capitalist engine" than the perfect competition which orthodox economics loves so dearly.

A second caveat is the following: how relevant is what either Engels or Schumpeter had to say about monopoly and trusts to the realities of contemporary capitalism? Do we not live in a world of increasing global competition, "trust-busting", and often real competition between domestic rivals, such as supermarket chains? Yes. But we also live in a world of mergers, of byzantine interrelationships between multinationals, where rivals may own parts of each other's concerns and where competitors co-operate in joint ventures. And big supermarket rivals, by their very size, can still indulge in the monopolistic practice of buying cheap from their suppliers and selling dear to the public. As J.K. Galbraith drily observed about anti-trust laws:

> these laws have not checked the great thrust to concentration and oligopoly. King Canute looks down on those who administer our anti-trust laws with the utmost understanding and sympathy. [12]

(5) *Collapse of the Capitalist Ethos* - Joseph Schumpeter has now nearly completed his journey to the House of Scientific Socialism. But he is getting there by an odd route, denying nearly every idea of the prophet and his disciples about the necessary collapse of the "capitalist engine". As we have just seen, even monopoly and imperfect competition can be turned to the advantage of the "capitalist engine" to deliver the goods in greater quantity and quality and at cheaper prices.

Where Marx saw capitalism inexorably concentrating into a sprinkling of fat cats surrounded by the penurious masses howling for justice, Schumpeter sees capitalism as spreading its bounty ever farther and wider to allow an ever-increasing mass comfort - a line of thought extending from Adam Smith through Lady Thatcher to Francis Fukuyama. But at this point in the journey, rather than joining the chorus in praise of individual enterprise and private property, Schumpeter veers off abruptly and dashes at last into the Marxist camp. It is the increasingly civilized life and comfort of the masses, bolstered by a Welfare State mentality, socialized by the very conditions of the modern "capitalist engine", that will lead - probably, finally - to the choice of a fuller socialist alternative as both more economically efficient and more humanly satisfying.

II The viability of central planning

In a 1949 lecture, "The March into Socialism", Schumpeter explains what he means by the socialist economic alternative:

> it is hardly possible to visualize a socialist society...without a huge bureaucratic apparatus that manages the productive and distributive process and in turn may or may not be controlled by organs of political democracy such as we have today ... Therefore we may equate the march into socialism to a conquest of private industry and trade by the state. The apparent paradox that this very same process is described by classic socialist doctrine as the 'withering away of the state' is easily resolved if we take account of the Marxist theory of government. Observe further that socialism does not exclude decentralized decision-making in the administrative sense - just as the central management of an army does not deny all initiative to commanders or subgroups. And observe finally, that socialism in our sense does not necessarily - that is, by logical necessity - exclude the use of competitive mechanisms as we see, e.g., from the Lange-Lerner model. Freedom of consumers' choice and of choice of occupation may, but need not necessarily, be restricted in socialist societies...
>
> I speak of centralist socialism only because it holds place of honor in the discussion. But other possibilities should not be neglected ... a development towards some form of guild socialism is not entirely off the cards. [13]

There are, for Schumpeter, two main objections to the viability of central planning to be answered. The first is an objection, most famously associated with the economist Ludwig von Mises, that declares that central planning cannot even *in principle* work, because, unlike the capitalist price-mechanism, it lacks any rational mechanism for allocating resources in production and distribution. The second is an objection, most famously associated with that icon of the New Right, Frederick von Hayek, that central planning will not *in practice* be successful because it will be too complicated to manage effectively.

Schumpeter explains the in principle objection in a passage which includes one of his many swipes at the "Marxist faithful":

> Starting from the proposition that rational economic behaviour presupposes rational cost calculations, hence prices of cost factors, hence markets which price them, he [von Mises] concluded that in a socialist society, since there would be no such markets, the beacon lights of rational production would be absent so that the system would function in a haphazard manner if at all. To this

> and similar criticisms or perhaps to some doubts of their own, the accredited exponents of socialist orthodoxy had at first not much to oppose except the argument that the socialist management would be able to start from the system of values evolved by its capitalist predecessor - which is no doubt relevant for a discussion of practical difficulties but not at all for the question of principle - or a paean on the miraculous glories of their heaven, in which it would be easy to dispense altogether with capitalist tricks like cost rationality and in which comrades would solve all problems by helping themselves to the bounties pouring forth from social stores. This amounts to accepting the criticism, and some socialists actually seem to do so even today. [14]

The solution to von Mises's criticism is, says Schumpeter, to be found in the economist Enrico Barone, building on hints contained in earlier work by von Wieser and Pareto:

> Both perceived that the fundamental logic of economic behaviour is the same in both commercial and socialist society from which the solution follows. Barone, a follower of Pareto, was the first to work it out. [15]

In a market society, rationality of both production and distribution are solved simultaneously. Production involves combining the factors of production (land, labour, capital) in the most rational (i.e., cost-effective) way. This is done by buying or hiring them on conventional supply/demand principles setting their price. Since this act is also what provides incomes, it conveniently settles the way that the social product will be distributed by the same stroke that it settles the way that the social product will be produced.

The two chief problems for a socialist society are that, on the face of it, (1) there are no market values for either production or distribution; and (2) even if there *were* market values for production, it would be anathema for a socialist society to allow principles of *distribution* to be settled in such a way, since it would violate the basic socialist principle of just distribution according to real human need rather than according to the "effective financial demand" of incomes arrived at by the price-mechanism of production.

So in a socialist society, distribution - or who gets how much of the social product - must be settled by a *political decision*. Schumpeter says:

> Distribution thus becomes a distinct operation and, in logic at least, is completely severed from production. This political act or decision would have to result from, and in turn go a long way towards determining, the economic and cultural character of the society, its behaviour, aims and achievements; but it would be completely arbitrary when viewed from the economic standpoint ... the commonwealth may adopt an equalitarian rule - and this again in any of the many meanings that may be associated with equalitarian ideals - or admit inequalities to any desired degree. It might even distribute with a view to producing maximum performance in any desired direction ... It may study the wishes of individual comrades or resolve to give them what some authority or other thinks best for them; the slogan 'to everyone according to his needs' might carry either meaning. But some rule must be established. [16]

Whatever rule of distribution is decided on, it is best met by issuing comrades with vouchers functioning as claims on goods and services provided by the socialist engine of production. It will be still more convenient if these vouchers

> express the claims not in goods but by equal amounts of conveniently chosen but meaningless units - we can call them simply units, or moons or suns or even dollars – and rule that units of each good will be handed over against the surrender of a stated number of them. [17]

Schumpeter continues:

> But the ministry need not fix the individual 'prices' except by way of initial suggestions. Given the tastes and the equal 'dollar incomes', comrades will reveal, by their reactions to these initial suggestions, at what prices they are ready to take the whole social product save those articles that nobody cares to have at all, and the ministry will then have to accept those prices if it wishes to have the stores cleared. [18]

But Schumpeter concedes that this does not fully resolve von Mises's objection:

> But of course this presupposes that a definite quantity of every good has been produced. The real problem, the solvability of which has been denied, is precisely how this can be done rationally, i.e., in a way which will result in a maximum of consumers' satisfaction subject to the limits imposed by the available resources, the technological possibilities and the rest of the environmental conditions. [19]

Schumpeter proceeds to fill in this gap:

> Suppose the board [central planning authority] rules that industrial managements can have any quantities of producers' goods and services they choose to call for subject to three conditions. First, they must produce as economically as possible. Second, they are required to transfer to the central board, for every unit of each producer's goods and services called for, a stated number of those consumers' dollars which they have acquired by previous deliveries of consumers' goods - we might just as well say that the central board declares itself ready to 'sell' to any industrial management unlimited quantities of producers' goods and services at stated 'prices'. Third, the managements are required to call for and to use such quantities as (and not less than), producing in the most economical manner, they can use without having to 'sell' any part of their products for less 'dollars' than they have to transfer to the central board for the corresponding amounts of the means of production. In more technical language, this condition means that production in all lines should be such as to make 'prices' equal (not merely proportional) to marginal costs. [20]

By such means, then, we have fitted production or supply to consumption or demand in every bit as rational a way as big business does in a commercial society:

> Exactly as today every firm in a perfectly competitive industry knows what and how much to produce and how to produce it as soon as technical possibilities, reactions of consumers (their tastes and incomes) and prices of means of

production are given, so the industrial managements in our socialist commonwealth would know what to produce, how to produce and what factor quantities to 'buy' from the central board as soon as the latter's ["market-clearing"] prices are published and as soon as consumers have revealed their 'demands'.[21]

This, then, in essence, is Schumpeter's answer to von Mises. But is it not something of a Pyrrhic victory? Has not Schumpeter in a sense *accepted* von Mises's objection in the very process of *answering* it? For he has only been able to answer von Mises by arguing that a rational form of central planning would, underneath it all, reproduce all the essential features of markets, which was von Mises's whole point.

Schumpeter deals with this objection succinctly:

> The cause of that family likeness is by now clearly visible ... our socialism borrows nothing from capitalism, but capitalism borrows much from the perfectly general logic of choice. Any rational behaviour must of course display certain similarities with any other rational behaviour ... If our historical acquaintance with economic phenomena had been made in socialist environments, we should now seem to be borrowing socialist concepts when analysing a capitalist process.
>
> So far, there is nothing for capitalist-minded economists to congratulate themselves on in the discovery that socialism could after all only use capitalist mechanisms and categories. There should be as little reason for socialists to object. For only the most naive mind can feel disappointed at the fact that the socialist miracle does not create a logic of its own, and only the crudest and most stupid variants of the socialist creed can be endangered by any demonstration to that effect - those variants according to which the capitalist process is a wild jumble without any logic or order at all. Reasonable people of both persuasions can agree on such resemblance as there is and remain just as far apart as ever.[22]

Analogously, we might argue that, viewed as means of transport, the horse and cart and the automobile must share inevitable similarities due to the "logic of transport". But it would be silly to conclude that they are therefore the same thing, and to further conclude that it would on that account be pointless to change from one to the other. The "superiority of the blueprints" - whether of horse and cart and automobile or of capitalist and socialist economics - will be decided by factors such as the comparative performance of each, their respective ability to resolve social problems, and so forth.

Schumpeter now moves on to addressing the other main objection to central planning - the von Hayek type objection:

> It consists of the 'practical impossibility' on which, it seems, most anti-socialist economists are at present inclined to retire after having accepted defeat on the purely logical issue. They hold that our central board would be confronted with a task of unmanageable complication. [23]

But Schumpeter argues that this objection can easily be overcome, because the von Hayek objection is already dealt with in answering the von Mises objection:

> our solution of the theoretical problem will satisfy the reader that it is eminently operational; that is to say, it not only establishes a logical possibility but in doing so also shows the steps by which this possibility can be realized in practice ... there is in this respect no very fundamental difference between socialist and commercial economies either as to the problems which the theorist meets in showing how an economic system proceeds to a state that could be 'rational' ...... or as to the problems which managers have to meet in actual practice. If we admit previous experience to start from as most socialists do....the task is of course greatly simplified, particularly if the experience is of the big business type. [24]

In fact, Schumpeter goes on, two big problems of commercial management will simply disappear in a socialist economy:

> A very important class of these [problems] consists ... in the uncertainties about the reaction of one's actual and potential competitors and about how general business situations are going to shape. Although other classes of uncertainty

> would no doubt persist in a socialist commonwealth, these two can reasonably be expected to vanish completely. The managements of socialized industries and plants would be in a position to know exactly what the other fellows propose to do and nothing would prevent them from getting together for concerted action.[25]

But might it still not be argued that the conditions of contemporary capitalism nevertheless reintroduce a return of the von Hayek objection about "workability", if not of the von Mises objection about "rationality"? A socialist planned economy of the type that Schumpeter envisages must entail effective control over a nation or region for its plan to work. What Schumpeter could not have foreseen is the "globalization" of industry, commerce, and finance which, just as it hinders the effective working of Keynesian-style control of national economies, would also hinder the effective control of a centrally planned economy. It has sometimes been said that global finance and multinational industry will punish any national capitalist government that even *thinks* about instituting a socialistic programme of nationalized industry. Does this not mean that in contemporary conditions, even if socialist central planning is an "abstractly rational option", it can no longer be a practically workable one?

This problem seems formidable, but it actually has several dimensions. In the first place, it is a *political* rather than an economic problem. What is really being said is that national governments no longer have sufficient political power over their "economic engines" to restructure them, even if it is the will of their people that they should do so. Should they be unwise enough to try nevertheless, the argument is that the pressures of the global economic system may punish them with economic hardship or even ruin (basically by such tactics as withdrawing capital and affecting currency value). All that a socialist economy could do in such circumstances would be to try to tough it out, like Cuba. This is a "complexity" that in the most real sense affects the "workability" - i.e., the practical possibility - of socialist planned economies. But it is not a "complexity of management" in the sense in which von Hayek originally castigated the "hopeless complication" of planned economies in practice. Rather, as Schumpeter might argue, if Nissan and General Motors can handle the extra complications added to their organization by multinational operations, then so too could a planned economy - and by much the same means: new developments in the technologies of communication, information, and transport.

Another issue which lurks here is highly speculative and perhaps fanciful. Marx, Engels, and Schumpeter all argued that it was the pressures provided by the "creative destruction" of capitalism that led to concentration and big business. It is not hard to see that those same pressures also led to contemporary "globalization". Now, just as Marx, Engels, and Schumpeter all argued that the transmutation into big business secretly contained the ingredients that make the transition to socialism easier, could it not be argued that the "global transmutation" secretly contains the ingredients that make the transition to global socialism easier? If there is anything in this rather fanciful hypothesis, it is easy to see how it might help solve one especially intractable problem: the problem of how a socialist nation or region can "go it alone" against the pressures of a capitalist world.

III The superiority of the socialist blueprint

(1) *Boosting of Productive Forces* - It cannot be emphasized enough how crucial it is to the whole Marxist project that socialist economics will "boost the productive forces" in a way impossible under capitalism, since capitalism is held by Marx to stifle the "full potential of productive forces" due to its mode of exchange for profit (a central "inner contradiction" of capitalism). If this does not happen, if human material welfare is not improved by such removal of scarcity, then, as Marx tells us in *The German Ideology*, we might as well forget about the revolution, comrades - because "all the old ugliness" will necessarily re-emerge, with divided humans selfishly scrabbling for as big a piece as possible of a small cake.

So Marx is championing a form of "growth economics" that goes beyond anything so far seen in capitalism. Leaving aside the fact that many environmentalists will denounce such a scheme as crazy and impossible, I want to ask whether Schumpeter too regards this "boosting of productive forces" as one of the chief superiorities of the socialist blueprint.

Given that Schumpeter is highly critical, as we have seen, of most of Marx's central ideas, it is not at all clear that he holds unambiguously to this central tenet of the Marxist faith. On the contrary, he believes that the "capitalist engine" is quite capable of removing "all the old ugliness" by boosting productive forces without any transition to socialism.

Nevertheless, there is some reason for thinking that Schumpeter agrees with Marx to an extent. For he says that suppose a socialist industry can produce the same amount more cost-effectively by the introduction of new technology. This would mean that it generated a "profit" or more "surplus value". Now it could return this "profit" to the central authority for investment or redistribution for the good of the comrades; or it could simply *produce more* for the comrades directly with the full original funds allotted by the central authority. In which case it would be fulfilling some of the great promise of socialist economics held out by Marx.

But several provisos should be made here. Marx, as much as any capitalist, holds that some portion of the social product must be retained for "fresh means of production", i.e., as "surplus value" or "savings and investment", rather than for producing more for immediate consumption. Without such investment, new technologies for even further boosting of productive forces would be unlikely to emergé. Also, if our socialism is to have any moral and international flavour, this may well mean that the comrades in New York, Paris, and London will have to tighten their belts a bit in order to allow the "profits" gained from their "surplus value" to be invested in the kind of economic projects that will allow the comrades in Sudan and Ethiopia to loosen their belts a bit.

Also, we should remember that Schumpeter holds that the "capitalist engine" is already doing all this, and will do so even more in the future: that most profits from "surplus value" are utilized not for the luxury consumption of a "few dividend-mongers" (or for arms for oppressive regimes), but for mass production and consumption on an ever wider and more cost-effective international scale. For that is how capitalists make money.

At the same time, to qualify the above point, Schumpeter also seems to believe that the benefits of even greater "concentration of capital", of being "super-big", of transmuting from big business capitalism to full socialism would *speed up* the "boosting of productive forces" and so, again, fulfil something of the Marxist promise.

(2) *Redistribution of Wealth* - It is, perhaps not unexpectedly, on the question of distribution of wealth that socialist economics holds out the greatest promise and is most clearly related to the central *moral* ideals of socialism (which Schumpeter hardly ever directly mentions) - the famous trinity of Liberty, Equality and Fraternity. The reason why this should be so is clear if we hark back to what Schumpeter says about how the logic of rational production in capitalist market economies simultaneously decides the logic of incomes and therefore the distribution of wealth. In the logic of socialist production, there is no such immediate link, and therefore there is no logical reason why wealth should not be distributed in a completely egalitarian manner by means of political rather than economic decision. The only thing, indeed, that would rationally prevent this is if some inequality of reward was required to act as an inducement for effective functioning of the productive and social system.

Schumpeter amusingly states some possibilities:

> the prestige motive, more than any other, can be molded by simple reconditioning: successful performers may conceivably be satisfied nearly as well with the privilege - if granted with judicious economy - of being allowed to stick a penny stamp on their trousers as they are by receiving a million a year. Nor would that be irrational. For, assuming that the penny stamp will impress the environment sufficiently to induce it to behave deferentially toward the wearer, it will give him many of the advantages for the sake of which he at present prizes the million a year. This argument loses nothing by the fact that such a practice would only revive a device which in the past has been widely used with excellent results. Why not? Trotsky himself accepted the Order of the Red Flag. [26]

The socialist *ethos* more easily allows the use of such inducements and rewards, whilst allowing the real work of Liberty, Equality and Fraternity in "bettering the human clay" to flourish through the practical device of equalizing incomes and improving public welfare services. Whereas in the capitalist *ethos*, it would be far harder to induce talented souls like Bill Gates, Rupert Murdoch, and Madonna to perform for the reward of a penny stamp on their trousers. Doesn't "supply-side economics" tell us exactly that? That the abilities to redistribute wealth through taxation in capitalism are limited?

(3) *Economic Crises and Business Cycles* - For Schumpeter, the deep-seated cause of economic crises and cycles of boom and recession - apart from more superficial causes like poor government financial policy and irresponsible speculative bubbles - is the series of "long waves in economic activity", each of which consists of an "industrial revolution" in itself, inevitably attendant upon the "creative destruction" of economics in alliance with technology. He says:

> These revolutions periodically reshape the existing structure of industry by introducing new methods of production - the mechanized factory, the electrified factory, chemical synthesis, and the like; new commodities, such as railroad service, motorcars, electrical appliances; new forms of organization - the merger movement; new sources of supply ... new trade routes and markets to sell in and so on ... While these things are being initiated, we have brisk expenditure and predominating 'prosperity' ... and while these things are being completed and their results pour forth we have elimination of antiquated elements of the industrial structure and predominating 'depression'. Thus there are prolonged periods of rising and of falling prices, interest rates, employment and so on, which phenomena constitute parts of the mechanism of this process of recurrent rejuvenation of the productive apparatus.
>
> Now these results each time consist in an avalanche of consumer goods ... although in the first instance they spell disturbance, losses and unemployment ... the capitalist process, not by coincidence but by virtue of its mechanism, progressively raises the standard of life of the masses. It does so through a sequence of vicissitudes the severity of which is proportional to the speed of the advance. But it does so effectively. [27]

For Schumpeter, a major superiority of the socialist blueprint is that he believes it would be capable - without losing any of capitalism's ability to continually reshape things and enhance material welfare by doing so - of managing the attendant vicissitudes and human misery in a far more effective manner. He says:

> Capitalist enterprise does not lack regulators ... But the planning of progress, in particular the systematic coordination and orderly distribution in time of new ventures in all lines, would be incomparably more effective in preventing bursts at some times and depressive reactions at others than any automatic or manipulative variations of the rate of interest or the supply of credit can be. In fact, it would eliminate the cause of cyclical ups and downs whereas in the capitalist order it is only possible to mitigate them ...
>
> And the whole of our argument might be put in a nutshell by saying that socialization means a stride beyond big business on the way that has been chalked out by it or, what amounts to the same thing, that socialist management may conceivably prove as superior to big-business capitalism as big-business capitalism has proved to be to the kind of competitive capitalism of which the English industry of a hundred years ago was the prototype. [28]

(4) *"Beefsteak Socialism" and a "Better Human Clay"* - I touch last on controversial issues regarding authoritarianism and democracy in the socialist blueprint, and on the equally controversial topic of "immediate wants" and "real human needs".

By "beefsteak socialism", Schumpeter means the problems attendant on democratically allowing the comrades to demand production of goods and services which satisfy their "immediate wants" (which, besides beefsteaks, may include heroin, pornography, bear-baiting, and gladiatorial circuses). And by a "better human clay", Schumpeter means the problems attendant on some authority or other (whether democratically chosen or not) commanding or persuading the comrades to improve their tastes and learn to be satisfied with the production of goods and services which it (and perhaps they?) believes to correspond with their long-term interests and "real human needs".

But put this way, we can see that the problem is not unique to socialism. Governments already command their citizens not to use heroin or to bait bears, and already try to persuade citizens to use cars less, to smoke less, and so forth. Also, as is well known, big business in market societies, through the use of clever advertising, may not only "manufacture wants" but go even further and try to persuade consumers that such manufactured wants are fulfilling "real human needs" (rather than fulfilling the "immediate wants" and functional needs of business and shareholders to make profits). If a socialist society were to find that the rationality of its economic system were threatened by difficulties in clearing its stocks of an unpopular (but worthy) good at a cost-effective price, then it could - but with rather more integrity - take a leaf out of commercial advertising's book. In trying to persuade the masses for health reasons to drink more Comrade-Cola and less gin, for example, it might even suggest in its propaganda campaign that everyone should want "to buy the world a Comrade-Coke", and that it would be a fine socialist act to drink the stuff, since it would "put the world in perfect harmony". If this still failed to convince, then it would have to take another leaf out of the capitalist book and innovate: providing a substitute good, equally worthy, but more popular with consumers. If all else failed - and the issue were important enough, as perhaps where environmental dangers were concerned - then it could resort to sheer command as a last alternative.

Notes

1. Joseph Schumpeter, *Capitalism, Socialism and Democracy*, George Allen & Unwin, 1987, p. 33.
2. Ibid., p. 33.
3. Ibid., p. 118.
4. Ibid., p. 118.
5. Ibid., p. 117.
6. Ibid., p. 70.
7. Ibid., pp. 34-35.
8. Ibid., p. 67.
9. Ibid., pp. 33-34.
10. Frederick Engels, *Socialism: Utopian and Scientific*, Swan Sonnenschein & Co. (London), 1907, trans. Edward Aveling, pp. 68-70.

11. *Capitalism, Socialism and Democracy*, p. 186.
12. J.K. Galbraith and N. Salinger, *Almost Everyone's Guide to Economics*, Penguin, 1978, p. 53.
13. *Capitalism, Socialism and Democracy*, p. 422.
14. Ibid., pp. 172-173.
15. Ibid., p. 173, ftn.
16. Ibid., pp. 173-174.
17. Ibid., p. 174.
18. Ibid., p. 174.
19. Ibid., p. 175.
20. Ibid., pp. 175-176.
21. Ibid., p. 177.
22. Ibid., p. 182.
23. Ibid., p. 185.
24. Ibid., pp. 185-186.
25. Ibid., p. 186.
26. Ibid., p. 208.
27. Ibid., p. 68.
28. Ibid., pp. 195-196.

4 Simone Weil and Marx: The Impossible Dream

Introduction

A friend of hers once said of Simone Weil that she understood the Crucifixion but she never really understood the Resurrection. Where Marx was concerned, it might be said that she largely believed his account of the Oppression but she never really believed his account of the Liberation. The thought of this extraordinary person - a unique mixture of Platonist, Christian mystic, and Marxist - is to be found in such works as *The Notebooks*, *The Need for Roots*, *On Science, Necessity and the Love of God*, and *Oppression and Liberty*.

It is on the last of these works that I wish to concentrate here, since it contains her most systematic evaluation of Marx - both of what she finds "of genius" about this "generous soul" and what she finds "puerile" about this "idolater". The essays and fragments contained in *Oppression and Liberty* were written between 1933 and 1943, shortly before she starved herself to death, and it is possible to detect a gradual shift of emphasis in them. In early essays, she is encouraging comrades in the workers' movement to revise those parts of Marx which she believes are no longer relevant to contemporary conditions, in the hope that "a more rational society" might still be possible. But, as the book moves on, it seems clear that her analysis of oppression and of flaws in Marxist doctrine and method make it impossible for her any longer to seriously believe in a revolution that could liberate the great mass of humanity.

In what follows, I divide the discussion into five parts: (1) Weil's Metaphysics: Gravity and Grace; (2) Natural and Social Oppression; (3) Two Impossible Dreams of Liberty; (4) Marx Right and Marx Wrong; (5) Conclusion.

I Weil's metaphysics: gravity and grace

Weil believed that there were two forces at work in the universe. She variously called them gravity and grace, matter and spirit, the power of force and the power of love, and, following Plato, the necessary and the good. She explains it thus:

> The central contradiction in human life is that man, with a straining after the good constituting his very being, is at the same time subject in his entire being ... to a blind force, to a necessity completely indifferent to the good. So it is; and that is why no human thinking can escape from contradiction. [1]

Yet this contradiction must somehow be mysteriously reconciled. So she tells us:

> As Plato said, an infinite distance separates the good from necessity. They have nothing in common. They are totally other. Although we are forced to assign them a unity, this unity is a mystery; it remains for us a secret. The genuine religious life is the contemplation of this unknown unity ...
>
> In this respect the whole of materialism, so far as it attributes to matter the automatic manufacture of the good, is to be classed among the inferior forms of the religious life ... Marxism is a fully-fledged religion, in the impurest sense of the word ... an opium of the people.
>
> For that matter, only a shade of difference, something infinitely small, separates a spirituality like Plato's from materialism. He does not say that good is an automatic product of necessity, but that spirit has dominion over necessity through persuasion; it persuades necessity to cause most of the things that take place to turn towards the good, and necessity is overcome by means of this wise persuasion ... We find the same conception in China, in India, in Christianity ... 'Our Father which is in secret'.
>
> The share of the supernatural here on earth is that of secrecy, the infinitely small...

> The decisive operation of the infinitely small is a paradox ... but nature, which is a mirror of the divine truths, everywhere presents us with images of it. Catalysts, bacteria, fermenting agents are examples. [2]

This is the mystic and Platonist in Simone Weil at its furthest remove from the Marxist in her. And such "mystical mumbo-jumbo" would no doubt be likely to raise the hackles of many Marxists, and of Marx himself. But as she moves towards her more concrete analyses of oppression and force, the affinities with Marx become clearer, as we shall see next.

II Natural and social oppression

Weil sets the scene for her analysis of oppression in a 1933 essay, "Prospects":

> No workers' State has ever yet existed ... except for a few weeks in Paris in 1871, and perhaps for a few months in Russia in 1917 and 1918. On the other hand, for nearly fifteen years now, over one-sixth of the globe, there has reigned a State as oppressive as any other which is neither a capitalist nor a workers' State. Certainly Marx never foresaw anything of this kind. But not even Marx is more precious to us than the truth. [3]

The terms "State capitalism" and "a workers' State with deformations" have often been used by Marxists to identify such entities as the Stalinist state. But Weil suggests there may be need to think beyond the categories of "capital" and "proletariat" bequeathed by Marx in order to grasp a new form of oppression, oppression by management or bureaucracy, a form of oppression maybe common to all complex industrial societies, whether they call themselves capitalist, socialist, fascist or anything else.

She elaborates on this theme in the central essay, "Reflections concerning the Causes of Liberty and Social Oppression". In an analysis that begins much like Rousseau's and Marx's, she shows how natural oppression - that is to say, humanity's subjection to nature - is relieved only at the cost of social oppression. The oppression is not *removed*; it is merely *transposed*:

> In short, man seems to pass by stages, with respect to nature, from servitude to dominion ... Unfortunately, this emancipation is only a flattering semblance ... instead of being harried by nature, man is henceforth harried by man. [4]

She adds:

> Marx clearly perceived this in connection with the State; he understood that this machine for grinding men down, cannot stop grinding so long as it goes on functioning, no matter in whose hands it may be. But this insight has a far more general application. Oppression proceeds exclusively from objective conditions. The first of these is the existence of privilege; and it is not men's laws or decrees which determine privileges, nor yet titles to property; it is the very nature of things. [5]

The reason why this is "the very nature of things" is as follows:

> In short, wherever, in the struggle against man or against nature, efforts need to be multiplied and coordinated to be effective, co-ordination becomes the monopoly of a few leaders as soon as it reaches a certain degree of complexity, and execution's primary law is then obedience; this is true both for the management of public affairs and for that of private undertakings. [6]

She goes on to concede that, in spite of this necessary division of functions, and therefore the necessity of privilege, oppression could still in theory be mitigated by "the resistance of the weak" and the "feeling for justice of the strong". But what makes this in practice impossible is the inevitability of the struggle for power. Again, in theory, one can conceive of two ways of breaking out of the struggle for power, although in practice, argues Weil, both are unrealizable:

> There are only two ways of breaking the circle, either by abolishing inequality, or else by setting up a stable power, a power such that there exists a balance between those who command and those who obey. [7]

But to dream of a stable power is impossible. On this point, Weil seems more consistent than Hobbes, who, whilst conceding that power is unstable in a state of nature, held to the vision of the stable power of a supreme sovereign. But this is not a real possibility, argues Weil:

> It would be otherwise if one man could possess in himself a force superior to that of many other men put together; but such is never the case; the instruments of power - arms, gold, magical or technical secrets - always exist independently of him who disposes them, and can be taken up by others. Consequently all power is unstable. [8]

Since power can never achieve its real object, which is to be finally and permanently in control of the ends to which it is a means, its very instability tends to make it also insatiable in maintaining and extending itself:

> Power, by definition, is only a means; or to put it better, to possess a power is simply to possess means of action which exceed the very limited force that a single individual has at his disposal. But power-seeking, owing to its essential incapacity to seize hold of its object, rules out all consideration of an end, and finally comes, through an inevitable reversal, to take the place of all ends. It is this reversal of the relationship between means and end, it is this fundamental folly that accounts for all that is senseless and bloody right through history. Human history is simply the history of the servitude which makes men - oppressors and oppressed alike - the playthings of the instruments of domination they themselves have manufactured, and thus reduces living humanity to being the chattel of inanimate chattels. [9]

Here again we see how Weil will sometimes take a point from Marx - such as Marx's account of how capitalism oppresses in different ways both the powerful and the powerless, making them playthings of their own instruments - and extend it more generally.

But if the dream of a stable power is idle, what of the other way of "breaking the circle" of power-struggles by "abolishing inequality", that is to say abolishing social oppression by abolishing the complexity of society which makes division of functions, obedience and command, caste and privilege necessary? The price to pay might be that any such simpler society would be more at the mercy of nature, but would it not perhaps be a price worth paying? Weil retorts:

> From time to time the oppressed manage to drive out one team of oppressors and to replace it by another, and sometimes to even change the form of oppression; but as for abolishing oppression itself, that would first mean abolishing the sources of it, abolishing all the monopolies, the magical and technical secrets that give a hold over nature, armaments, money, co-ordination of labour. Even if the oppressed were sufficiently conscious to make up their minds to do so, they could not succeed. It would be condemning themselves to immediate enslavement by the social groupings that had not carried out the same change; and even if this danger were to be miraculously averted, it would be condemning themselves to death, for, once men have forgotten the methods of primitive production and have transformed the natural environment into which these fitted, they cannot recover immediate contact with nature. [10]

Here, then, we see how Weil - in an argument that is not dependent on her metaphysical views - isolates why she believed in Marx's account of oppression, but not his account of liberty. Marx wanted two incompatible things: all the advantages of social dominion over nature without the disadvantages of inequalities in social power; all the "monopolies, the magical and technical secrets that give a hold over nature" without the division of labour, the specialization, the castes and classes, the command and obedience that, on Weil's analysis, must inevitably accompany it. In this respect, Weil would presumably have found Hegel's account of things more realistic. Hegel, in the *Philosophy of Right* in a typically "fluid" account, could be seen as basically trying to explore how Rousseau's ideals of the good society based on Liberty, Equality and Fraternity could be made relevant to large, complex, industrializing societies rather than to small, simple, agrarian societies. Hegel's account is notoriously hard to pin down along the orthodox political spectrum, since his "fluid synthesis" can justly be seen as containing elements of liberalism, socialism, fascism, and conservatism. Hegel's answer to the question of how one could manage to combine all the advantages of a complex society (with necessary division of labour, bureaucracy, caste and privilege) with "true equality" was to distinguish between "Civil Society" and "State" and between "particular" and "universal" consciousness. In short, at the level of everyday economic and social activity (the level of particular individuals functioning in Civil Society), inequality was inevitable. But at what Hegel called the "most rational level" of the "true individual" possessed of "universal State consciousness", all the different parts of Civil Society allowed equality to be regained in the greater whole. That is to say, no matter if the particular individual is a toilet cleaner or a bank president, no matter if their different functions necessitate inequality of power and wealth and prestige, they are both equal citizens of the State, comrades fraternally bound together in the joint enterprise of the State, equal in rights before the law, each doing their bit for the common good according to their respective stations and duties. Just as in an army, the necessary division of functions and the need for discipline, command and obedience requires differences of rank, power, and prestige, yet these particular differences are superficial in comparison with the "universal consciousness" of the "spirit of the regiment". "All for one and one for all".

Marx famously criticized this attempt of Hegel's to "update Rousseau" as cosmetic and as a confidence trick - a mere appearance of equality induced in the masses by false consciousness. Real equality, for Marx, required the abolition of social and economic inequality at the level of Civil Society, a removal of classes, not a smothering of class-conflict at the level of "State consciousness".

Simone Weil no doubt agreed with Marx that Hegel's attempt to "magic away" the oppression attendant on class-divisions was no more than an ideological confidence trick. But her own analysis of oppression also makes it clear that she would have agreed with Hegel against Marx that any attempt to realize the Marxist vision of a classless society where political oppression had "withered away" was, if anything, a still more dangerous "opium of the people". The attempt to force together the two incompatibles of a complex, organized, bureaucratic, industrialized society that was yet truly classless and self-governing could only end in more oppression, or chaos, or an unhappy mixture of both - to Robespierre's Reign of Terror, to Stalinism, to Mao's Cultural Revolution or to even more grotesque experiments such as Pol Pot's Year Zero.

Hegel's own analysis is contained in the "Absolute Freedom and Terror" section of *The Phenomenology of Spirit*, expressing his disillusionment with the French Revolution. In the light of Weil's account of the instability of power, Hegel's analysis is very much to the point, since, underneath it all, he is arguing that the attempt to *organize* a complex, classless society *must inevitably lead to more instability of power and more oppression*, since it is a contradiction in terms between the "universal will" (the classless, democratic, self-governing aspect) and the "government" (the necessity for a governing class that claims to embody and express the General Will in its bureaucratic organization and actions). As Hegel puts it:

> The relation, then, of these two, since each exists indivisibly and absolutely in itself, and thus cannot dispose of a middle term which would link them together, is one of wholly *unmediated* pure negation, a negation, moreover, of the individual as a being *existing* in the universal. The sole work and deed of universal freedom is therefore *death*, a death too which has no inner significance or filling, for what is negated is the empty point of the absolutely free self. It is thus the coldest and meanest of all deaths, with no more significance than cutting off a head of cabbage or swallowing a mouthful of water.
>
> In this flat, commonplace monosyllable is contained the wisdom of the government, the abstract intelligence of the universal will, in the fulfilling of itself. The government is itself nothing else but the self-established focus, or the individuality, of the universal will. The government, which wills and executes its will from a single point, at the same time wills and executes a specific order and action. On the one hand, it excludes all other individuals from its act, and on the other hand, it thereby constitutes itself a government that is a specific will, and so stands opposed to the universal will; consequently, it is absolutely impossible for it to exhibit itself as anything but a *faction*. What is called government is merely the *victorious faction*, and in the very fact of its being a faction lies the direct necessity of its overthrow; and its being government makes it, conversely, into a faction, and so guilty. When the universal will maintains that what the government has actually done is a crime committed against it, the government, for its part, has nothing specific and outwardly apparent by which the guilt of the will opposed to it could be demonstrated; for

> what stands opposed to it as the *actual* universal is only an unreal pure will, *intention*. *Being suspected*, therefore, takes the place ... of being guilty. [11]

Now, I suppose that it could be argued that all Hegel - and by implication, Weil - are doing here is dramatically exaggerating the kind of healthy tensions that are bound to exist, and ought to exist, in any complex, bureaucratic society that calls itself democratic - tensions between the people and the government, and between factions or parties denouncing each other as "unrepresentative of the will of the people". All this poetic talk about "death", "suspicion" and "guilt", it might be said, could be read as just a fancy way of talking about the invaluable element of instability of power by which, in a democracy, governments are replaced by winning or losing *elections*.

However, this would be to misrepresent the essential point that both Hegel and Weil are trying to make: the more a political philosophy, such as Marxism, aims at ideals of liberty, equality, fraternity, democracy and self-government, the more difficulties will its leaders and bureaucratic coordinating organizations face. *For, by definition, they already shouldn't exist.* Hence they are bound to find themselves on the defensive, both in regard to the people and to rival factions claiming to represent the "true General Will" as well as the "undiluted message of Marx". Hence their need to maintain and extend their power by every means of persuasion and force; hence the increased bitterness and intensity of power-struggles; hence the climate of fear, suspicion, the midnight knock on the door and the secret police. In short, under such conditions, ironically intended to *remove* oppression, oppression is bound to *increase*.

Simone Weil, then, can be seen as finally separating herself from those Marxists who claim that "true Marxism" has never been tried, and that unfortunate historical accidents have led to faulty experiments with Marxism in societies too "unripe" for it. Rather, she holds to the view that "true Marxism" never could be tried, due to the contradictory requirements inherent in Marxist doctrine: a demand for classless equality and self-government that is incompatible with an equally insistent demand for a complex, technological, bureaucratic and specialized society. As such, she is obviously of the persuasion who believe that, if you start off with Marx, you should not be at all surprised that you end up variously with Stalin, Mao, Caescescu and Pol Pot.

III Two impossible dreams of liberty

It is clear that while Simone Weil shared some of Hegel's ideas about why complex organization and classless equality were not a happy combination, she had no truck with Hegel's solution - that the inequalities and class-struggles of Civil Society could be *aufgehoben* ("suspended and absorbed") in the "higher consciousness" of the State. She obviously regarded this as a confidence trick, just as Marx did. Instead, in her outline of the "good society", she looks to the utopian, decentralized strand in Marx's thought. In the section of "Reflections concerning the Causes of Liberty and Social Oppression" pointedly called "Theoretical Picture of a Free Society", she says:

> Perfect liberty is what we must try to represent clearly to ourselves, not in the hope of attaining it, but in the hope of attaining a less imperfect liberty than is our present condition; for the better can be conceived only by reference to the perfect. One can only steer towards an ideal. [12]

In fact, she explores two possible versions of utopia - one which she regards as possibly attainable, but not worth the attaining, and so dystopian rather than utopian; the other which she regards as truly utopian, both in the sense of being definitely worth attaining but incapable, because so perfect, of being attained.

I shall deal first with her arguments about the false utopia - that of the technical utopia of an automated leisure society. Although she does not completely rule out the practical possibility of attaining such a state of things, she does point out that there may very well be real limits to this technocratic dream. The limits are of three main sorts: technological limits, ecological limits, and limits imposed by the struggle for power. So she says:

Aristotle admitted that there would no longer be anything to stand in the way of the abolition of slavery if it were possible to have the indispensable jobs done by 'mechanical slaves', and when Marx attempted to forecast the future of the human species, all he did was to take up this idea and develop it. It would be true if men were guided by considerations of welfare; but ... the senseless demands made by the struggle for power have taken away even the leisure for thinking about welfare. The raising of the output of human effort will remain powerless to lighten the load of this effort as long as ... the methods of labour and of warfare give to a few men a discretionary power over the masses; for the fatigue and privations that have become unnecessary in the struggle against nature will be absorbed by the war carried on between men for the defence or acquisition of privilege. Once society is divided up into men who command and men who execute, the whole of social life is governed by the struggle for power, and the struggle for subsistence only enters in as one factor, indispensable to be sure, of the former. [13]

Anyway, even were such a technical utopia attainable, it would not be humanly liberating in any real sense:

We have only to bear in mind the weakness of human nature to understand that an existence from which the very notion of work had pretty well disappeared would be delivered over to the play of the passions and perhaps to madness... A nation of idlers might well amuse itself by giving itself obstacles to overcome ... but the efforts that are the result of pure whim do not form for a man a means of controlling his own whims ... The only liberty that can be attributed to the Golden Age ... is in reality an unconditional surrender to caprice. The human body can in no case cease to depend on the mighty universe in which it is encased; even if man were to cease being subjected to material things and to his fellows by needs and dangers, he would only be more completely delivered into their hands by the emotions which would stir him continually to the depths of his soul and against which no regular occupation would any longer protect him.[14]

Against this false view of liberty and utopia, Weil contrasts a true view of liberty and deduces a utopia from it:

> True liberty is not defined by a relationship between desire and its satisfaction, but by a relationship between thought and action; the absolutely free man would be he whose every action preceded from a preliminary judgment concerning the end which he set himself and the sequence of means suitable for attaining this end. [15]

The utopia which she deduces from this definition of liberty has much in common with the utopian, decentralized strand in Marx, his emphasis on self-government, and his pronouncements concerning the "degrading division between manual and intellectual labour", on which Weil sets great store. She also in many ways looks back to Rousseau's decentralized ideal of the small community of equal citizens, and, implicitly, to Plato's ideas of the degrees of knowledge, from mere befuddlement to received, uncritical opinion to the fullest, comprehensive understanding of things.

Utopia, for Weil, would therefore be a society which had work at its centre, where all work was as far as possible informed by thought and creative problem-solving, in a community small and integrated enough so that everyone could participate in an informed way regarding its decisions. The following three extracts convey the flavour of her ideal society:

> Men would ... be bound by collective ties, but exclusively in their capacity as men; they would never be treated by each other as things. Each would see in every work-fellow another self occupying another post, and would love him in the way that the Gospel maxim enjoins. Thus we should possess, over and above liberty, a still more precious good; for if nothing is more odious than the humiliation and degradation of man by man, nothing is so beautiful or so sweet as friendship. [16]

> a team of workers on a production-line under the eye of a foreman is a sorry spectacle, whereas it is a fine sight to see a handful of workmen in the building trade, checked by some difficulty, ponder the problem each for himself, make various suggestions for dealing with it, and then apply unanimously the method conceived by one of them ... At such moments the image of a free community appears almost in its purity. [17]

> Social relations would be directly modelled upon the organization of labour, men would group themselves in small working collectivities where co-operation would be the sovereign law, and where each would be able to understand clearly and to verify the connection between the rules to which his life was subjected and the public interest. [18]

The reasons why such a free society must remain purely theoretical have already been explained by Weil (see Part II). In the light of this, what can be done? Nothing very much, according to Weil. At times her conclusion is one of resigned despair:

> In such a situation, what can those do who still persist, against all eventualities, in honouring human dignity both in themselves and in others? Nothing, except endeavour to introduce a little play into the cogs of the machine that is grinding us down; seize every opportunity of awakening a little thought wherever they are able; encourage whatever is capable, in the sphere of politics, economics or technique, of leaving the individual here and there a certain freedom of movement amid the trammels cast around him by the social organization. That is certainly something, but it does not go very far. On the whole, our present situation more or less resembles that of a party of absolutely ignorant travellers who find themselves in a motor-car launched at full speed and driverless across broken country. When will the smash-up occur after which it will be possible to consider trying to construct something new? Perhaps it is a matter of a few decades, perhaps of centuries ... It seems, however, that the material resources of our civilization are not likely to become exhausted for some considerable time, even allowing for wars; and, on the other hand, as centralization, by abolishing all individual initiative and all local life, destroys by its very existence everything which might serve as a basis for a different form of organization, one may suppose that the present system will go on existing up to the extreme limit of possibility. [19]

At other times, the resignation seems even more complete, although touched with more compassion for everyone involved, as in the conclusion to her essay "Meditation on Obedience and Liberty":

> The social order, though necessary, is essentially evil, whatever it may be. You cannot reproach those whom it crushes for undermining it as much as they can; when they resign themselves to it, it is not through strength of character but, on the contrary, as the result of a humiliation which extinguishes the virile qualities in them. Neither can you reproach those who organize it for defending it, or make them out to be forming a conspiracy against the general welfare. The struggles between fellow citizens do not spring from a lack of understanding or goodwill; they belong to the nature of things, and cannot be appeased, but can only be smothered by coercion. For anyone who loves liberty, it is not desirable that they should disappear, but only that they should remain short of a certain limit of violence. [20]

IV Marx right and Marx wrong

If we ask what Simone Weil admired about Marx, the answer is something as follows: she admired his moral indignation and thirst for justice; she admired certain "ideas of genius" which he introduced, which no one has bettered, and which are perennial truths as valid today as ever; she admired the brilliance and accuracy of his application of those ideas to the society of his own time; she admired what she called his "philosophy of labour" - that is, his view that fulfilling work was a necessary ingredient of the good life and mindless and monotonous work an obstacle to it.

So she tells us:

> Marx was a generous soul. The sight of injustice made him suffer really, one might say in his flesh. This suffering was intense enough to have made it impossible for him to live had he not harboured the hope of an imminent and earthly reign of complete justice. For him, as for many, need was the best of proofs. [21]

> Marx was the first and, unless I am mistaken, the only one - for his researches were not followed up - to have the twin idea of taking society as the fundamental human fact and of studying therein, as the physicist does in matter, the relationships of force.

Here we have an idea of genius, in the full sense of the word. It is not a doctrine; it is an instrument of study, research, exploration ..." [22]

Marx's truly great idea is that in human society as well as in nature nothing takes place otherwise than through material transformations. 'Men make their own history, but within certain fixed conditions'. To desire is nothing; we have got to know the material conditions which determine our possibilities of action; and in the social sphere these conditions are defined by the way in which man obeys material necessities in supplying his own needs, in other words, by the method of production. [23]

Marx's really outstanding work is the application of his method to the study of the society around him. He defined with admirable precision the relations of force in that society. [24]

Two things in Marx are solid, indestructible. One is the method which makes society an object of scientific study by seeking to define therein relationships of force; the other is the analysis of capitalist society as it existed in the nineteenth century. The rest not only is not true but is even too inconsistent, too empty, to be called erroneous. [25]

What, then, are these empty, inconsistent untruths with which Weil charges Marx? In essence, I think they boil down to the one all-encompassing charge: Marx uses his praiseworthy moral indignation and thirst for justice to quite illegitimately, and with a high degree of gullibility, twist his "idea of genius" - the study of relationships of social force - to his desired ends: a society of free, equal, self-governing beings who have managed to achieve release from natural scarcity and oppression without becoming ensnared in social oppression and power struggles.

To this basic charge, Weil adds another metaphysical criticism which I think is not only unnecessary to her main argument, but possibly even harmful to it. She maintains that a large part of the reason why Marx made his mistake was because he, being a materialist "idolater", was unaware of the huge distance separating force from justice, necessity from the good, gravity from grace.

So she tells us:

Being unable to work out a doctrine, he [Marx] seized upon the two beliefs most current in his time ... the cult of science and utopian socialism.

In order to adopt them together, he gave them a fictitious unity by means of formulas which, if one enquires into their meaning, eventually fails to reveal any, except a sentimental state of mind ... The less meaning a formula possesses, the thicker is the veil drawn over the illegitimate contradictions of a line of thought.

This does not mean ... that Marx ever set out intentionally to deceive the public. The public he had to deceive in order to be able to live was himself. [26]

Actually, Marx gives a first-rate account of the mechanism of capitalist oppression; but so good is it that one finds it hard to visualize how this mechanism could cease to function ... as long as there is, on the surface of the globe a struggle for power ... the workers will be exploited ... What Marx assumed, without however proving it, was that every kind of struggle for power will disappear on the day socialism is established in all industrial countries. [27]

The power which the bourgeoisie has to exploit and oppress the workers lies in the very foundations of our social life ... Thus the workers' complete subordination ... is founded on the factory organization and not on the system of property ...

Marx had clearly perceived that State oppression is founded on the existence of organs of government that are permanent and distinct from the population, namely, the bureaucratic, military and police machines; but these permanent organs are the inevitable result of the radical distinction existing ... between the managerial and executive functions. [28]

Before even examining the Marxist conception of productive forces, one is struck by the mythological character it presents in all socialist literature, where it is assumed as a postulate. Marx never explains why productive forces should tend to increase ... In the same way, why is it that, when social institutions are in opposition to the development of productive forces, victory should necessarily belong beforehand to the latter rather than the former? Marx evidently does not assume that men consciously transform their social conditions in order to improve their economic conditions; he knows perfectly well that up to the present social transformations have never been accompanied by any clear realization of their real long term consequences; he therefore implicitly assumes that productive forces possess a secret virtue enabling them to overcome obstacles. Finally, why does he assert without demonstration, and as a self-evident truth, that the productive forces are capable of unlimited development?

The whole of this doctrine, on which the Marxist conception of revolution entirely rests, is absolutely devoid of any scientific basis. [29]

The great mistake of the Marxists and of the whole of the nineteenth century was to think that by walking straight on one mounted upwards into the air. [30]

V Conclusion

Weil's criticisms of Marx strike me as very mixed in their strength as arguments. I conclude by trying to assess the validity of her criticisms over five main areas: (1) the Marxist "mythology" of productive forces; (2) the condemnation that the Marxist explanation of war is "puerile"; (3) the charge that Marx's depiction of the working class as "debased cogs" in the capitalist machine gives him no reason to hope that such cogs could constitute a revolutionary, self-governing force; (4) her condemnation of Marx's materialist "idolatry" in terms of her own metaphysics of matter and spirit; (5) her analysis of oppression.

(1) Her criticism that Marx's "mythology" of productive forces has no rational foundation strikes me as weak - and also as inconsistent with some of her other analyses. Surely, in his analysis of capitalism, which Weil admired, Marx rationally explains both why the forces of production should tend to increase and yet simultaneously stifle their full potential. The answer in both cases is the search for profit. This analysis of Marx's has nothing to do with "mystical propensities of productive forces" and everything to do with the actions of the most powerful social groupings upon matter and upon society. Similarly, it is Marx's explanation of the

very unforeseen and unintended consequences of the actions of the most powerful group (capitalists) which leads to the increasing "immiseration" of the "industrial reserve army" and the perceived possibility of a more rational form of political economy. Again, the reason why, when productive forces come into conflict with existing social institutions, the former tend to triumph is not because of any mystical properties that Marx illegitimately ascribes to productive forces, but because real political and economic power comes more and more to belong to the social group which dominates the new productive forces, rather than to the social group which dominates existing social institutions - hence the industrial bourgeoisie replace the feudal aristocracy, the organized and educated working class replace the troubled bourgeoisie. I do not see how Marx's account can be called incoherent or irrational or "mythological" on this score. One can certainly say that history has not always proved him correct.

Weil's accusation that Marx's belief in an almost unlimited development of productive forces is Panglossian is a much stronger argument - and one with which most contemporary environmentalists would agree.

(2) I find her arguments that Marxist explanations of war are superficial are much stronger - especially when bolstered by her analysis of oppression and the struggle for power. Marx takes hold of one very true point - that many human conflicts revolve round the struggle for scarce resources - and tries to make that point bear more weight than it is capable of. The idea that the removal of scarcity - if universal - would give humanity one less thing to quarrel about is a good one; the idea that it would remove all causes of strife really does seem facile. If Weil's analysis of oppression has any merit, tensions between rulers and ruled, between rival factions and parties, and between rival collectivities seem inevitable. Perhaps, as Weil says, for those who love liberty it is not desirable that such disputes should disappear, but only that they "remain short of a certain limit of violence".

Hegel, in spite of his unfortunate glorification of war, did have one very pragmatic argument about why the complete disappearance of war was unlikely - an argument that applies equally whether we are talking about nation states, federations or confederations, or self-governing communes. In the *Philosophy of Right*, he wrote:

There is no Praetor to judge between states; at best there may be an arbitrator or mediator, and even he exercises his functions contingently only, i.e., in dependence on the particular wills of the disputants. Kant had an idea for securing 'perpetual peace' by a League of Nations to adjust every dispute. It was to be a power recognized by each individual state, and was to arbitrate in all cases of dissension in order to settle them. This idea presupposes an accord between states; this would rest on moral or religious or other grounds and considerations, but in any case would always depend ultimately on a particular sovereign will and for that reason would remain infected with contingency. [31]

(3) Another line of criticism which Weil levels at Marx revolves round the argument that since Marx graphically portrays the condition of the masses under capitalism as that of "mindless cogs", it is unreasonable for him to expect the masses to be capable of becoming self-governing. While this argument may not be worthless, it does conveniently ignore those other aspects in Marx which emphasize the increasing education, political awareness and unity of the workers and also his candid admission of the difficulties of the period of "socialist transition".

(4) Many of Weil's criticisms depend for their force on the truth of her own metaphysical views. I find these criticisms to be from one point of view weak and from another point of view, if we accept the truth of her metaphysical views, to be actually self-defeating. The main thrust of these metaphysical arguments is to try and demonstrate that the materialist idolater Marx, since he was solely concerned with social relations of *force*, had absolutely no way of showing how such relations of force could lead to the *good*, since, in Weil's words, "an infinite distance separates the necessary [force] from the good". As a result of his flawed metaphysics, Weil sees Marx as duping himself by allowing his "sentimental state of mind" to illegitimately construct under a metaphysical cloud of verbiage the instrument of "scientific socialism". In Weil's eyes, it is an empty instrument, which nevertheless allows Marx to deceive himself into thinking that the *good* (the "utopian socialist" aspirations of his "generous soul") can be arrived at by the *force* of historical *necessity* (the nineteenth century cult of science, industry and progress). Hence, the gullible prophet

believes that, "by walking straight on", humanity will miraculously "mount upwards into the air" and achieve utopia.

The weakness of Weil's argument here, which claims that the materialist is wrong in "attributing to matter the automatic manufacture of good", can be seen by the fact that, as a piece of dogmatic metaphysics, her argument will cut no ice with anyone who dogmatically holds to a rival metaphysics. For a naturalist like David Hume, for instance, or for evolutionary naturalists (of whom Marx is surely a variant), the good comes precisely from nature, and so Weil's criticism weighs nothing.

Even more problematically, if we take Weil at her word, and assume the truth of her metaphysics of gravity and grace, then it seems that this will allow us to bridge the gap between the necessary and the good, between force and justice, that she finds such a deficiency in Marx's materialism. For it will allow us to introduce an element of Providence into the Marxian account. I have already quoted Weil in Part I as telling us that "Spirit persuades necessity to cause most of the things that take place to turn towards the good, and necessity is overcome by means of this wise persuasion."

(5) I leave to last what I think is easily Weil's strongest criticism of Marx - her analysis of oppression (see Part II). The crux of her criticism here is to identify an "inner contradiction" within the Marxist project of liberation: an incompatibility between its desire for a complex, industrialized, progressive, necessarily bureaucratic society and its simultaneous desire for freedom, equality, democracy and self-government. In spite of Marx's famous pronouncement that *praxis* can reconcile what seem unresolvable contradictions in ideas, Weil can see no way of squaring this particular circle. And it is this criticism of Weil's that is the most damning and needs most serious consideration.

I add one last point. For Weil, writing at a time when the centralizing forces of corporate capitalism, Stalinism and Nazism were engulfing individuals, it was the oppression of the individual by the central bureaucratic authority that was the chief danger. Today, while this is still so, many commentators are emphasizing a new source of oppression. With the collapse of Soviet authority in the aftermath of the Cold War, and the partial withdrawal of the USA from zones of influence, there are those, like Michael Ignatieff in *The Warrior's Honor*, who argue that a new source of oppression is occurring in many parts of the globe. This is the oppression resulting from a sort of Hobbesian anarchy and lawlessness that is overtaking regions with collapsing states or states too weak to allow their bureaucratic, military and police machines to exercise real control over all their territories. Oppression can spring from too weak a state as well as from too strong a one.

This was an irony of history that one could not expect either Marx or Simone Weil to foresee. But, in any analysis of oppression and liberty, centralization and decentralization, authority and accountability, and in any depiction of the "good society", it is one that needs to be taken into account.

Notes

1. Simone Weil, *Oppression and Liberty*, trans. R. Wills and J. Petrie, Routledge & Kegan Paul, 1972, p. 173.
2. S. Weil, Ibid., pp. 174-175.
3. S. Weil, Ibid. p. 6.
4. S. Weil, Ibid., p. 63.
5. S. Weil, Ibid., p. 63.
6. S. Weil, Ibid., pp. 64-65.
7. S. Weil, Ibid., p. 66.
8. S. Weil, Ibid., p. 67.
9. S. Weil, Ibid., p. 69.
10. S. Weil, Ibid., pp. 69-70.
11. G.W.F. Hegel, *The Phenomenology of Spirit*, trans. A.V. Miller, Oxford U.P., 1977, p. 360.
12. S. Weil, *Oppression and Liberty*, p. 84.
13. S. Weil, Ibid., pp. 70-71.
14. S. Weil, Ibid., pp. 84-85.
15. S. Weil, Ibid., p. 85.

16. S. Weil, Ibid., p. 100.
17. S. Weil, Ibid., p. 101.
18. S. Weil, Ibid., p. 106.
19. S. Weil, Ibid., p. 121.
20. S. Weil, Ibid., p. 146.
21. S. Weil, Ibid., p. 172.
22. S. Weil, Ibid., p. 172.
23. S. Weil, Ibid., p. 45.
24. S. Weil, Ibid., p. 161.
25. S. Weil, Ibid., p. 164.
26. S. Weil, Ibid., p. 170.
27. S. Weil, Ibid., p. 40
28. S. Weil, Ibid., pp. 41-42.
29. S. Weil, Ibid., pp. 43-44.
30. S. Weil, *Gravity and Grace*, Routledge & Kegan Paul, 1952, p. 153.
31. G.W.F. Hegel, *Philosophy of Right*, trans. M. Knox, Oxford U.P., 1967, pp. 213-214.

5 If I Ruled the World: "the Kitchens of the Future"

Introduction

Marx was reluctant to provide "blueprints for utopia" or "recipes for the kitchens of the future". He seems to have had two main reasons for this: (1) it was neither his task nor his wish to play at "If I ruled the world" and to tyrannically tell free people how to organize the good society; for, by definition, if they were free, that was their own task; (2) anyway, providing blueprints for utopia was bound to be fruitless, since it ignored the historical limits of the blueprint-maker's own vision: it would be as futile as asking a prehistoric person for a realistic vision of possibilities in the year 2000.

Both are good arguments; but both have their flaws. In the first place, because Marx only gave vague hints and guesses about the good society, he must surely accept some of the responsibility for the use to which some of his professed followers put his ideas. In the second place, since he seems to have believed that proletarian revolution was imminent in the industrialized world, the "historical limits" argument is less convincing, and all the more reason for requiring rather more definite recipes for the kitchens of the future. Thirdly, the mixture of vagueness and failed projects of putting Marxism into practice not unnaturally leads the sceptical to wonder whether Marx is not now completely irrelevant as a thinker.

To be fair, Marx did provide *some* fairly definite general principles. In the sphere of economics, since he believed that capitalism's "inner contradictions" would eventually render it unviable, and since in his mind 'capitalism' was synonymous with 'market', it seems that his vision had to insist on doing away with markets, replacing them with a "more rational form of economics" where planning would be paramount. Proper planning would be both fairer and more efficient than the market, and would crucially be a mixture of central coordination and decentralized autonomy. In the sphere of politics, the same basic principle would apply: the non-oppressive classless society would require central coordination yet decentralized autonomy. So his master-idea for the good society, unsurprisingly for a dialectician, was this idea of "centralization within decentralization". It was as if he were telling his future followers: "Centralization within decentralization is the key. Don't stray from that. But by all means try every possible experiment in combining these two things freely for yourself. You can, if you wish, go on 'particularizing' this 'universal' requirement endlessly, 'relativizing' this 'absolute' forever, until you find your own best formula for your own historical, technological, and social conditions".

Of course, Marx himself was prepared to 'relativize' this 'absolute' requirement in fairly definite terms when it came to the period of imminent "socialist transition". Here, the emphasis would have to be quite strongly on the 'centralization' part of the procedure, at least till the battle was finally over with the class enemy. So he tells us in *The Communist Manifesto*:

> These measures will of course be different in different countries.
>
> Nevertheless, in the most advanced countries, the following will be pretty generally applicable:
>
> 1. Abolition of property in land and application of all rents of land to public purposes.
>
> 2. A heavy progressive or graduated income tax.
>
> 3. Abolition of all right of inheritance.
>
> 4. Confiscation of the property of all emigrants and rebels.
>
> 5. Centralization of credit in the hands of the State, by means of a national bank with State capital and an exclusive monopoly.
>
> 6. Centralization of the means of communication and transport in the hands of the State.
>
> 7. Extension of factories and instruments of production owned by the State; the bringing into cultivation of wastelands, and the improvement of the soil

generally in accordance with a common plan.

8. Equal liability of all to labour. Establishment of industrial armies, especially for agriculture.

9. Combination of agriculture with manufacturing industries; gradual abolition of the distinction between town and country, by a more equable distribution of the population over the country

10. Free education of all children in public schools. Abolition of children's factory labour in its present form. Combination of education with industrial production, etc., etc. [1]

At the end of Chapter 2, I concluded that Marx's economic analyses still had relevance to contemporary global capitalism. But I also concluded that that inevitably left anyone convinced of this with three problems: (1) Planning versus Market; (2) Utopian and Scientific Socialism; (3) Environmental Limits and Constraints.

The first problem is whether it can be shown that there is a viable form of planned economy that would improve on contemporary capitalism without reproducing or making worse its economic imperfections and social injustices. The second problem is whether there are any real historical forces at work in the contemporary world that could make the world a better place. The third problem is how environmental limits impinge on growth economics.

One reason for looking in some detail at Joseph Schumpeter and Simone Weil is that both do, in their different ways, provide answers to these three problems. The other reason is that both of them, while highly critical of Marx, nevertheless derive tremendous value from his ideas.

I divide what follows into four parts: (1) Schumpeter's Answer; (2) Weil's Answer; (3) If I Ruled the World; (4) Contemporary Forces.

I Schumpeter's answer

Schumpeter clearly concentrates on the centralization aspect of Marxism, although, to be fair, he does say that a movement towards a more decentralized guild socialism is not impossible, and he does argue that centralization need not totally dispense with initiative, autonomy, and competition at lower levels of the chain of command.

The strength of Schumpeter's analysis seems to me to lie in the following areas: (1) he dissolves the market versus planning controversy by persuasively arguing that it is in many respects a pseudo-controversy, since both must obey a similar logic of economic rationality; (2) in the same argument he also shows how the "logistical complexity" of socialist planning need not be much more complicated than the existing complexities of big business; (3) he shows how socialist planning can more easily permit of egalitarian redistribution of income and provision of public services than capitalism; (4) he argues with some degree of plausibility that cooperative planning could better cope with the instabilities caused by the "creative destruction" of capitalism; (5) he at least offers the hope of "a better human clay" through socialism.

The weakness of Schumpeter's analysis, I think, lies in three main areas: (1) it is unclear how central planning can be viable in a world where global forces of capital have semi-deliberately sought to evade its political possibility; (2) no very effective answer is given to the question of what "stick" and "carrot" would replace the "discipline of the market"; (3) although Schumpeter says that political authority "may or may not" continue to be democratic, it is clear that his analysis of what he sees as a *realistic* democracy is a very attenuated form where the uninformed masses are free only to vote for informed competitive elites who make all the real decisions on the people's behalf; typically, Schumpeter's arguments on this score are not without insight:

> What strikes me most of all and seems to me to be the core of the trouble is the fact that the sense of reality is so completely lost. Normally, the great political questions take their place in the psychic economy of the typical citizen with those leisure-hour interests that have not attained the rank of hobbies, and with subjects of irresponsible conversation...
>
> This reduced sense of reality accounts not only for a reduced sense of responsibility but also for the absence of effective volition ... He is a member of an unworkable committee, the committee of the whole nation, and this is why he expends less disciplined effort on mastering a political problem than he expends

on a game of bridge ...

Thus the typical citizen drops down to a lower level of mental performance as soon as he enters the political field He argues and analyzes in a way which he would readily recognize as infantile within the sphere of his real interests. He becomes a primitive again. His thinking becomes associative and affective. [2]

Nevertheless, Schumpeter's realism here would seem to lead him precisely into the trap which Simone Weil diagnoses as the main problem with Marxism: inevitable oppression of the individual by bureaucracy. For this kind of reason, many have referred to Schumpeter, the "imperious Austrian" with his centralist, elitist tendencies, as a "bourgeois Marx".

With less justice, some have labelled Schumpeter a "bourgeois Marx" on the grounds that his socialism admits no revolutionary force of change. This is unfair, since Schumpeter's account here is every bit as "scientifically socialist" as that of Marx and Engels. It is the very development of productive forces, and the changes that this development brings about in the minds of people, that will produce, for Schumpeter, a socialist ethos. It is just that Schumpeter does not realistically see how this can avoid a large element of rule by bureaucratic elites. On this score, Weil would agree with him. But while Schumpeter can regard such an outcome with optimism, Weil can only regard it with despair.

On the topic of environmental limits and constraints, Schumpeter, in the light of today's worries about global warming and ozone layer depletion, is less than satisfactory. As when he tells us:

the decreasing rate of increase in population removes from the range of practical considerations the idea that nature's response to human effort either already is or must soon become less generous ... Technological progress effectively turned the tables on any such tendency, and it is one of the safest predictions that in the calculable future we shall live in an *embarras de richesse* of both foodstuffs and raw materials, giving all the rein to expansion of total output that we shall know what to do with. [3]

Weil, although writing at roughly the same time as Schumpeter, is altogether more circumspect about how environmental limits and constraints will affect the Marxist - and the capitalist - project of "removing scarcity".

II Weil's answer

I argued that, in the sphere of both economics and politics, Marx had a vision of dialectically fusing together the two apparent opposites of centralization and decentralization, social coordination and local and individual autonomy. If Schumpeter concentrates on the centralization aspect, Simone Weil just as obviously concentrates on the decentralization aspect. For her, true socialism can only mean that each individual exercises some real control over their economic and political life. And, for her, this must mean that social units must be small enough for each person to properly *understand* the full range and complexity of that life, and so be able to make informed decisions and/or to be able to judge the decisions of anyone claiming to represent the community.

As we have seen from her "Theoretical Picture of a Free Society", this is the ideal "to steer towards". But, as we have also seen from her analysis of oppression and power, just this is what is impossible, and for that reason Marxism is largely a fraud - an "opium of the people". All her strongest arguments turn on this one point: you cannot square the circle of "centralization within decentralization"; you cannot simultaneously have all the advantages of a complex, stratified society (the condition of power over nature) without the corresponding disadvantages of individual powerlessness and bureaucratic control. Hence the oppressed can only change their form of oppression; they can never be truly free, in the sense of having real control over their lives.

For Weil, as for Hegel, this situation was further aggravated by the fact that, in any society based on the ideals of Liberty, Equality and Fraternity, the legitimacy of any government - faction - was always suspect, and this very instability of power would tend to lead the government to try and exercise, ever more subtle and all-encompassing power and control. "After Freedom comes the Terror".

Did Marx have a way out of this vicious circle? Yes, but I think it has to be conceded that, on basic questions of freedom and authority, he never managed to think any further than Locke and Rousseau. We can read Locke as offering a way through the horns of Hobbes's dilemma about government: either we have freedom combined with undesirable anarchy ("the war of all against all") or we have sovereign authority which may tyrannically abuse us (Weil's bureaucratic oppression). Locke changed the terms of this dilemma by arguing that if all of us join together as the sovereign authority, making our own laws and agreeing to be bound by them, then we can avoid the undesirable consequences of each horn of the dilemma: there is no lack of coordination, order and control, yet there can be no tyranny, since we are ruling, through our elected representatives, over ourselves. We have thus, in broad outlines, what Weil declares impossible: a complex, stratified, coordinated society that is self-governing and autonomous. Further, the very element of instability of power is used to keep power stably with the people through the device of periodic elections. The stability of the power of the people is ensured through their ability to periodically remove any elected government who dissatisfies them. So the instability of power of their representatives is actually what ensures the stability of power of the people.

What does Rousseau add to this outline of Locke's? Basically, he argues that, if power of the people is not to be a sham, then it must fulfil several further conditions. Firstly, it would be a fuller democracy if all the people *directly* participated in making their own laws at Assemblies rather than *indirectly* through representatives. Secondly - and this seems to me his most important contribution - something approaching a "classless society", with no great divisions of wealth, status, power and prestige, would go a long way to ensuring that the interests of each individual (the "particular will") coincided with the interests of all individuals (the "will of all") and the common good (the "general will"). As Rousseau puts it:

> Do you want coherence in the state? Then bring the two extremes as close together as possible; have neither very rich men nor beggars, for these two estates, naturally inseparable, are equally fatal to the common good; from the one class come friends of tyranny, from the other, tyrants. [4]

Thirdly, Rousseau - mirroring a requirement of Weil's for the good society - thought it necessary that the society be small enough and simple enough for each person to properly understand its functioning. This would enable direct participation, informed decisions and problem-solving, and encourage comradeship.

It is not clear that Marx ever managed to think beyond a combination of Locke and Rousseau when it came to the *political* organization of his communist society or added anything genuinely new to their ideas. For instance, his famous slogan that "the free development of each will be the condition for the free development of all" seems to me to merely repeat Rousseau's central argument that in a classless society individual and social interests are more likely to coincide.

Does any of this answer Weil's criticisms about the inevitability of bureaucratic oppression? Well, it certainly *modifies* them in three ways. (1) Locke's basic scheme shows how the instability of power can be used to form a virtuous rather than a vicious circle of power-struggles - the instability of power of the representatives is what ensures the stability of power of the people, avoiding the worst excesses of both anarchy and tyranny. (2) Rousseau's emphasis on a classless society, with no great gap between incomes, at least mollifies the inevitable differences in power and status in a complex society with division of functions. (3) Rousseau's - and Weil's - emphasis on the need for an *informed* citizenry at least mollifies some of the gap between those who command and those who obey, and allows people to act on their knowledge when it comes to deciding powers at elections and referendums. The device of an election manifesto is also useful here.

There is one sphere, however, in which Marx very definitely thought beyond Locke - the sphere of economics. If Locke had shown the way out of the Hobbesian dilemma in regard to politics, we may see Marx as arguing that, in the sphere of economics, Locke is content to leave things resting precisely on *both* horns of the Hobbesian dilemma. Not only was capitalism a form of *tyranny* (of capital over labour), it was also a form of creative/destructive *anarchy* (the war of all against all of competing capitals). Taking his clue from Rousseau, Marx proceeded to argue that to make *political* democracy real, it was necessary to introduce *economic* democracy: there would be neither tyranny nor anarchy if the means of production and distribution were ruled, either directly or through representatives, by the people for the people.

III If I ruled the world

SPECTRE OF MARX: What was your first act as world ruler? I hope it was to resign and give power back to the people.
I: No, that was my second act. But first I offered some suggestions.
S of M (scornfully): Suggestions! Ineffectual utopian ramblings, do you mean!?
I: Well, it could be ... But as Simone Weil said, we can only conceive the better by reference to the perfect. We can only steer towards an ideal.
S of M (kindly): Ah, Weil was a generous soul. The sight of injustice made her suffer really, one might say in her flesh ... But what were these suggestions of yours?
I: They were quite simple really. First of all, I suggested to the world that no one had yet dreamed up a better ideal for the human race than universal Liberty, Equality and Fraternity. So I suggested that we adopt it as an ideal and shape our politics around it. Then I asked for objections.
S of M: And were there any?
I: Yes, there were several. The first was from GARLIC.
S of M: GARLIC?
I: Yes, God Against Revolution and Liberty Instead of Castes. They all argued that their sacred doctrines forbade them following my scheme, since their religion ordained inequality and castes. Some said this was the Will of God; some said it was the law of *karma*. So I asked them what their central beliefs were. Some said it was "Love God and love your neighbour as yourself"; some said it was "overcoming egocentricity and universal compassion". I said that these beliefs seemed more compatible with socialist ideals than with castes and inequality. They didn't seem to have any good arguments against that.
S of M: Who else was there?
I: There was FOBCOC - Friends of Burke and Conservative Organic

Communities. They said that communities were best left to evolve of themselves and that my idea was bound to end in tears. They cited Burke on the French Revolution; they cited Hayek; they even cited Rosa Luxemburg and Simone Weil on bureaucratic oppression. They declared that my ham-fisted utopianism would only succeed in robbing people of cherished, traditional liberties and destroying ages-old close-knit communities that were maybe quite happy with their social inequalities. I had to concede that these FOBCOC folk had half a point. So I suggested that maybe a compromise was possible. Any such existing conservative community - whether a hunting-gathering society, a monarchy, or a theocracy - should be asked if they actually *wanted* to remain as they were. If they said yes, then they should be left alone as much as was feasible. But if they answered along the lines of saying "We don't much like it, but we're powerless to change things", then it would be reasonable to assume that something - maybe a ruling class, maybe their own ignorance of other possibilities - was bamboozling them.

S of M: Hmm ... a bit naive, perhaps. Do we really need such rural idiocy? And, more fundamentally, these folk would have to change anyway. Things don't stand still. Men make their own history, but under conditions which are not of their own making.

I: Yes, but I was trying to be true to your idea of giving power to the people, letting *them* decide how best to organize their lives. And I was also trying to accommodate what truth there seemed to me to be in Burke's idea that people respond better to change when they institute it themselves and at their own rate, so that it seems to evolve naturally.

S of M: Fundamentally, it turns on the "centralization within decentralization" problem. Your heart may have been in the right place. But tell me, were there any other objectors?

I: Well, there were howls of rage from FOP (Friends of Postmodernism) and DERRUDA (Deconstructive Enemies of Reason, Revolution, Universality, Dialectic and the Absolute). They accused me of every kind of intellectual fascism. Hadn't I ever heard of "alterity" or "respect for the otherness of the other"? Was I really so naive as to believe in Reason, Progress and the "possibility of a pure presence uncontaminated by the trace of its own ineluctable other"? So I asked these folk where they stood.

There was such a jabber of voices that it was hard to decipher. Some declared that they didn't stand anywhere because there was nowhere safe to stand. Some declared that there were so many meanings to everything that it was the same as an ultimate meaninglessness. Some seemed no more than poseurs with nothing much to say about anything. Some seemed utterly confused and determined to try and confuse everyone else. The most intelligent of them seemed to be raising many of the points raised by Simone Weil, although usually without her clarity or passion: how social progress inevitably led to social oppression in one form or another; how "meta-narratives" of liberty - like your own - could contain the seeds of even greater oppression, how scientific and social progress, in solving one problem, merely raised numerous new problems. Some, again like Weil, said there were insoluble contradictions in human life that no amount of reason or social or scientific progress could eradicate. As a result they were very sceptical about the ideas of reason and progress. Some declared themselves to be the only true friends of democracy and justice, on the grounds that, having shown how every attempt to produce justice somewhere produced injustice somewhere else, and how every attempt to make democracy all-inclusive only succeeded in newly excluding or marginalizing some group or other, they had made people more aware about democracy and justice. Some seemed to believe that they had advanced the cause of democracy and justice in the very act of showing how difficult it was to ever achieve democracy and justice.

S of M: And what did you say to these to these professors?

I: I said to them that they didn't in principle seem *opposed* to my scheme of universal Liberty, Equality and Fraternity, it was just that, like Weil, they didn't think it was *realizable* in practice. So the answer to them was the same answer that Simone Weil gave to herself: we can only steer towards an ideal. I also remarked that Hegel had scornfully analyzed the sort of "beautiful soulism" to which many of them seemed to be prone - the idea that, because everything is so complex and morally ambiguous, no positive actions or policies are possible. Finally, I reminded them that you yourself were aware of the dangers of those who set out in search of Liberty, Equality and Fraternity actually ending up with Infantry, Cavalry and Artillery.

S of M: All the old filthy business reproducing itself? Yes, it's the crucial question of scarcity, you see. But, tell me, did anyone else raise objections?

I: Yes, there were a number of groups who were opposed to my scheme on principle, since they held to opposing ideals like inequality, power, authority, or plain selfishness. They included FOF (Friends of Fascism), POP (Politicians of Power), and IDARSBY (I'm Doing All Right, So Bugger You). I decided that the best way to reason with them was in the terms that they understood best. So I told them: "There's 5% of you and 95% of us. Are you sure that you want to argue with us? Because I think you're going to lose".

S of M: Now there I think you made a big mistake.

I: But there was no other way of reasoning with them!

S of M: That's not quite what I meant. I meant that I think you got your percentages wrong and that you failed to understand the relations between these groups and everyone else. Also you neglected one important category. Once again, it's the critical question of scarcity.

I: How do you mean?

S of M: Looking down on your contemporary global conditions, what I see is the following: a number of people belonging to the group you call IDARSBY and a larger number belonging to a category which you neglected to mention - INDSWSWO (I'm Not Doing So Well, So Watch Out). Both these groups have intimate relations, implicitly or explicitly, with FOF and POP, who promise to protect each group against the other. That's the main reason why the world is currently seething with tensions and bristling with military hardware, to say nothing about every kind of political and economic machination. Many of the people to whom you put your idea probably genuinely thought that they agreed with you. But that was because - as our friend Schumpeter puts it - they were thinking in an infantile way. What they really meant was that they liked the sound of your Liberty, Equality, Fraternity idea so long as it didn't really cost them anything. But what really matters to them is protecting their own interests.

I: But surely it was you yourself who pointed out that for the first time there *was* the possibility of a universal Liberty, Equality and Fraternity that need not cost anybody, because for the first time the technical conditions for removing scarcity were available?

S of M: Yes, but who listens to me anymore? When your contemporaries bother to think about the future at all, they either optimistically assume that the global market will eventually raise world-wide living standards, while preserving inequalities, or they pessimistically assume that the planetary environment will collapse under the strain. In the second case, especially, all the more reason for squabbling over scarce resources and jostling for advantage at someone else's expense. But we'll return to this question later. For now, tell me some more about your utopian agenda.

I: Well, my next suggestions concerned the whole question of decentralization and centralization. Politically, as I've already said, I didn't think that you or anyone else had managed to think further than a mixture of Locke and Rousseau. Therefore the broad outlines of political organization were pretty obvious. A *universal* Liberty, Equality and Fraternity obviously required some centralization, something approaching global government and a system of international law. The decentralization requirement means that any such global government was subject to replacement at periodic elections. The same system would apply at the level of the regions. At the level of the smallest units of political communities, more direct participation should be possible. Another way of getting some direct participation into the system might be as follows: a percentage of both global and regional government could be decided by lot rather than by election. So any citizen of the world might find themselves, as a result of this lottery, required to participate directly either in global or regional government. Not only would this be an analogon of something that already exists - selection for jury service - but it would be the closest that one might feasibly come to the Marxist requirement that every pastry cook should be capable of governing the state. Finally, the way that the regional and smaller communities chose to govern themselves would be their own affair, so far as it didn't conflict with global policy and international law.

Much the same scheme of centralization within decentralization would apply in the economic sphere. But here Rousseau's most important amendment of Locke - the need to abolish the gap between rich and poor - and your own developments of this idea of Rousseau's would be central. The centralizing task, at the global level, would simply be to manage overall supply and demand, its amount, its nature, and its development, in consultation with each main region.

S of M: Who would own the means of production and distribution?

I: Everyone. Every person in the world. But each region would hold its own territory in gift from the world, and each smaller community would hold its own territory in gift from its region. As for how each region and smaller community conducted their own economic affairs, that would be their own political decision, just so long as it didn't conflict with international economic policy and didn't infringe on international law concerning permissible differentials between highest and lowest income. Within these constraints, you could have competitive market mechanisms, pure command mechanisms, or any mixture of the two. This versatility of political and economic mechanisms would probably lead to more originality and innovation, would be useful for comparison, and would come closest to fulfilling the requirements of decentralization and self-government.

S of M: Everyone would be required to work, of course?

I: Yes, but as little as possible, at least where the work concerned was not something they were undertaking for their own fulfilment. For, in that case, of course, their "work" would also be their "play". The right perspective on the whole controversy about work and leisure seems to me as follows. Everyone needs time off, just to take it easy and have fun, whether they love their work or hate it. But no one hates work *per se.* They only hate boredom, drudgery, and stress. So the obvious goal is to make necessary work as pleasant and interesting as possible and to allow each individual to use at least part of their leisure to do their own fulfilling "work", the kind of thing they involve themselves in voluntarily out of interest or enthusiasm.

There's also another reason why leisure is a necessity. It's necessary in order to be a good citizen. My whole utopian scheme of centralization within decentralization falls to the ground unless it can fulfil four conditions: *education, information, transparency,* and *accountability.* Everyone should be able to play at "If I ruled the world". There is no other way of meeting Simone Weil's requirement for the good society that "each would be able to understand clearly and to verify the connection between the rules to which his life was subjected and the public interest". Unless citizens have enough leisure to educate themselves and to acquire necessary information, government activity ceases to be either transparent or accountable. Nor could the idea of a percentage of citizens, selected by lot, participating directly in government be more than tokenism. In fact, if the above conditions can't be fulfilled, or at least approximated to, the whole democracy would be tokenism; it would amount to no more than Schumpeter's elitist democracy where the ignorant masses are free only to vote for the informed elites who manage world affairs in theory on their behalf.

For much the same reason, if you don't have education, information, transparency and accountability, not only is your *liberty* pretty constricted, but you can't really expect to have much *fraternity*. For fraternity to be possible, citizens need to know and understand each other. While political and economic equality of freedoms can go a long way towards producing fraternity, you need more than that if you are to avoid hostility or the "enforced fraternity" of an oppressive central power. It was for this kind of reason that political thinkers like Rousseau emphasized small communities as best for fulfilling the conditions for fraternity: if you are to love your neighbour, the state needs to be small enough to know your neighbour.

S of M: But in your grand global utopia, surely just this is what would be impossible?

I: Yes, but it could at least be approximated to in a more real way than in Rousseau's time. Because, as you yourself might say, the technical conditions now exist to make it more of a reality - especially television and interactive media. It is imaginative use of these technologies that can make government more transparent and accountable - both by televizing crucial meetings and debates and by interactive assemblies, for instance. The same technologies can be used for the purposes of fraternity, so that citizens in all parts of the world can better know and understand each other. All this already happens, but in a very minimal way. And all this is based on the idea that the best way to avoid hostility, oppression, chaos or confusion is to set up the conditions where these things are least likely to occur. And these conditions are Liberty, Equality, Fraternity, centralization within decentralization, education, information, transparency and accountability. Exactly these principles would also apply to whatever military organization was necessary: it would be a question of the best trade-off between separation of power, balance of power, accountability and transparency of power, and effectiveness. So, whether we are talking about political, military or economic power, the same principles apply to them all.

S of M: Yet so far you've said nothing about what strikes me as the most critical question of all: the removal of scarcity. I still maintain that that the chief reason for human conflicts and for "class struggles" is this question of scarcity. Without removing scarcity, all talk of Liberty, Equality and Fraternity is in fact Idleness, Emptiness and Pomposity. Without it, any superficial change in social, political or economic relations will be trivial, since all the old ugliness will simply re-emerge, with divided humans squabbling for as big a slice as possible of a limited cake. I really believe that, in spite of Weil's protestations, my chief contribution was to hint at how it might be possible to remove scarcity in a way that need not cost anyone anything.

I: And the champions of capitalism have adopted your ideas (or accused you of adopting theirs). While the champions of the environment have cried a plague on both your houses. It seems to me that one of your leading ideas (which is also the idea of thinking capitalists) is that if everyone has more than enough of everything, then the major source of human conflict will disappear, since there need be no more struggle over scarce resources.

S of M: Yes, but put that way, you're travestying my position. I never meant that, for instance, if you own a Rolls Royce, and your neighbour has two, and you want a third, that kind of situation was possible or desirable. I meant that people should be sensible enough to distinguish between real needs and superfluous wants. Otherwise one simply opens the door to the madness of endless wasteful consumerism and infinite unsatisfiable wants.

I: Well, then, the chief factors in the equation are these: *economic growth, distribution of wealth, ecological sustainability*. The chief economic question of a global utopia is simply how best to balance these three factors so as to come closest to the goal of providing everyone with enough - or more than enough - of what they really need.

S of M: With the proviso that real needs are not completely static. For instance, you've indicated that in your utopia sophisticated communications media would be a vital need, not a superficial want. The economic and political coherence of your utopia would seem to depend on it.

I: Since 'wealth' and 'capital' are only terms that conveniently summarize actual planetary resources, actual artefacts and institutions, and the sum of human ingenuity, the economic direction seems pretty obvious: one aims at organizing human effort and ingenuity in such a way as to maximize planetary resources in the most efficient and sustainable way to create enough wealth to allow of an equable distribution that would satisfy everyone's real needs.
S of M: Will you resign now?

IV Contemporary forces

It might seem odd to conclude a book whose main thrust, however critical, is to argue for the continuing relevance of Marx's thought with an appeal to the ideas of a person who seems to have so little time for Marx. The person in question is the political philosopher and historian John Gray, who has made his opposition to Marxian theory and practice pretty clear. Gray is opposed to Marx's theory on the grounds that it is an instance of the deluded "Enlightenment Project" of trying to imperialize the globe with a universal reason and a universal civilization. He also holds that attempts to put this theory into practice have inevitably led to tyranny and oppression and the inefficiencies and corruption of central planning. In this second regard, especially, his view partly resembles the strictures of Simone Weil concerning "bureaucratic oppression".

Yet in my estimation Gray probably grasps contemporary historical forces better than any other current thinker. He also has a superb knack of drawing together all the various strands - economic, political, historical, cultural, philosophical, ecological - which make those forces what they are. I do not think I can improve on Gray's insights; but I can perhaps put them into a fuller perspective in regard to Schumpeter (for whom Gray avows his respect) and to Marx (for whom Gray seems to have so little respect).

After a flirtation with New Right ideas, Gray's political philosophy seems to have developed into a synthesis which is in many ways as hard to pin down as Hegel's: there are strong elements of the Postmodernist criticism of the "Enlightenment Project" of universal reason and civilization; there are strong elements of a (connected) Burkean Conservatism, with an emphasis on the limits of abstract reason and the need to respect "organic communities" and their different cultural needs and traditions; there is a strong ecological awareness; there is an appeal to the kind of tolerant, pluralist democratic liberalism of the Isaiah Berlin variety - a world that is a harmonious "coat of many colours".

All the above elements come together in Gray's book *False Dawn: the Delusions of Global Capitalism.* Gray conveniently summarizes the overall argument into eight main strands, as follows:

> [1] The free market is a construction of state power ... Since the natural tendency of society is to curb markets, free markets can only be created by the power of a centralized state ... [2] democracy and the free market are competitors rather than partners ... The normal concomitant of free markets is not stable democratic government. It is the volatile politics of economic insecurity ... [3] socialism as an economic system has broken down irretrievably. In both human and economic terms, the legacy of socialist central planning has been ruinous ... [4] though the implosion of Marxian socialism has been welcomed ... as a triumph of free market capitalism, it has not been followed in most formerly communist countries by the adoption of any western economic model ... [5] Marxism-Leninism and free-market economic rationalization have much in common ... [they both] adopt a Promethean attitude to nature and exhibit scant sympathy for the casualties of economic progress. Both are variants of the Enlightenment project of supplanting the historic diversity of human cultures with a single, universal civilization ... [6] The global free market is an American project ... global *laissez-faire* is not a conspiracy of corporate America. It is a tragedy ... in which a hubristic ideology runs aground on enduring human needs that it has failed to comprehend ... [7] A contradiction has emerged between the preconditions of an intact bourgeois civilization and the imperatives of global capitalism ... the chronic insecurities of late modern capitalism ... corrode some of the central institutions and values of bourgeois life ... [8] In the absence of reform, the world economy will fragment as its imbalances become insupportable ... As global *laissez-faire* breaks up, a deepening international anarchy is the likely human prospect. [5]

Why has "globalization" happened? Gray's sense of history leads him to say that globalization is not a new phenomenon while also maintaining that the degree and the rate of it in the contemporary world *are* unprecedented. This is due especially to the development of information technologies and their use in communication and techniques of production.

Why has global *laissez-faire* capitalism happened, as evidenced in the policies of international organizations like GATT, the IMF and the WTO? Gray presumably would not disagree with the "orthodox explanation" of both Left and Right that global *laissez-faire* had much to do with an attempt to restore capitalism's viability (and especially American capitalism's) by tilting the balance of power back towards capital from labour; nor perhaps would he be averse to Robert Brenner's thesis of "competing capitals" (both of which explanations I dealt with in Chapter 2). But what Gray does maintain is that the full explanation is more culturally complex. As he says, "the global free market is an American project", but at the same time it is not *merely* "a conspiracy of corporate America". It has deeper cultural roots, being partly a manifestation of the USA's popular vision of itself as the "true way forward" or the "last best hope for mankind". This has led to an uncritical equation of human freedom and democracy with free markets, the kind of equation argued for in such books as Francis Fukuyama's *The End of History and the Last Man*.

Unfortunately, says Gray, this equation is almost the reverse of the truth, since free markets are actually destructive of many features of democratic institutions and values, undermining especially one of the basic requirements that any people demands of any government: the need for stability and security. Gray points to contemporary America itself as evidence of this truth: massive inequality, seething tensions, a climate of fear and insecurity, the dismantling of Roosevelt's New Deal welfare legislation, the maintenance of social order through a scheme of mass imprisonment and zero-tolerance policing. The exporting of this "American Way" globally, via the USA's clout in institutions such as GATT and the IMF is not a happy prospect.

Here Gray appeals approvingly to the ideas of Joseph Schumpeter. He tells us:

> Joseph Schumpeter understood capitalism better than any other twentieth century economist. He saw that it did not work to preserve the cohesion of society. Left to itself it could well destroy liberal civilization. That is why he accepted that capitalism must be tamed. Government intervention was needed to reconcile the dynamism of capitalism with social stability. The same is true of global markets today. [6]

In the light of Schumpeter's actual arguments (see Chapter 3, "Schumpeter and Socialism: Big is Beautiful"), Gray's reading of Schumpeter here might seem rather selective and cavalier in pressing Schumpeter's ideas into the service of Gray's own arguments. On my understanding, the whole point of the "heretical twist" that Schumpeter gives to Marxist ideas is to argue that the "capitalist economic engine" will transform itself fairly painlessly from within, evolving finally into a bureaucratic socialism of (probably) the centrally planned variety. ' For Schumpeter, writing in the 1940s, this is how bourgeois, liberal, individualistic values will be overcome by a more collectivist, socialist ethos. Gray's reading of Schumpeter seems, ironically, actually closer to the orthodox Marxist account of the development of capitalism towards "increasing immiseration". All the more so when Gray draws analogies between the precarious plight of the nineteenth century proletariat and the insecurity of the late twentieth century middle classes under the "gale of creative destruction" of global markets.

Nevertheless, even if Gray might be accused of making rather creative use of Schumpeter's ideas, he does so with insight. As when he goes on to say:

> Today's believers in worldwide *lassier-faire* echo Schumpeter without comprehending him. They believe that by promoting prosperity free markets advance liberal values. They have not noticed that a global free market engenders new varieties of nationalism and fundamentalism even as it creates new elites. By eating away the foundations of bourgeois societies and imposing massive instability on developing countries, global capitalism is endangering liberal civilization. It is also making it harder for different civilizations to live in peaceful coexistence. Global *laissez-faire* has become a threat to peace between

states. The present international economic system contains no effective institutions for conserving the wealth of the natural environment. The risk is that sovereign states will be drawn into a struggle for control of the earth's dwindling natural resources. In the coming century ideological rivalries between states may well be succeeded by Malthusian wars of scarcity. [7]

Or again:

What is beyond serious doubt is that organizing the world economy as a single global free market promotes instability. It forces workers to bear the costs of new technologies and unrestricted free trade. It contains no means whereby activities that endanger the global ecological balance can be curbed... Organizing the world economy as a universal free market is, in effect, staking the planet's future on the supposition that these vast dangers will be resolved as an unintended consequence of the unfettered pursuit of profits. It is hard to think of a more reckless wager.

Yet the replacement of global *laisser-faire* by a managed regime for the world economy is, at present ... Utopian. Such a regime could be established only by the world's great economic powers acting in concert, and conflicts of interests make cooperation for any purpose more ambitious than crisis-management almost impossibly difficult. The necessary consensus on means and ends in policies on population control and environmental conservation does not exist. [8]

Nevertheless, Gray identifies historical forces that will undermine the "Washington consensus" of global *laissez-faire*:

With the steady banalization of new technologies the sources of power in the late modern period are flowing away from the western countries. As countries that were pre-industrial develop their own varieties of capitalism they are becoming less willing to submit themselves to the Washington consensus.

If China is successful in modernizing its economy it will play hardball with transnational organizations that attempt to enforce an American free trade agenda on it. So will Russia. The forces of the expanding world economy will break through the institutions of the global free market.

Global *laissez-faire* is a moment in the history of the emerging world economy, not its endpoint. Either the present regime will evolve into something its architects could scarcely have envisaged and certainly do not intend, or its institutions will become ineffectual and marginal. [9]

But the fact that there are historical forces working against the global free market does not of itself ensure that these forces are pushing the world economy into the more "planned" or "managed" or "governed" format that seems to be required on all fronts - political, economic, ecological and simply human. These historical forces may merely act to replace one kind of anarchic world with another. As Gray puts it:

> The likelihood must be that the *laisser-faire* regime will not be reformed. Instead it will fracture and fragment, as mounting scarcities of resources and conflicts of interest among the world's great powers make international cooperation ever more difficult. A deepening international anarchy is the human prospect.
>
> Will the resources of critical rationality which we have inherited from the Enlightenment enable us to cope with the disorders that its most recent project has created or compounded? Or is the global anarchy in which we find ourselves an historical fate against which we are bound to struggle, but which we are powerless to overcome?
>
> The spread of new technologies throughout the world is not working to advance human freedom. Instead it has resulted in the emancipation of market forces from social and political control. By allowing that freedom to world markets we ensure that the age of globalization will be remembered as another turn in the history of servitude. [10]

Gray does hold out a few shreds of hope that there may be historical forces working in a saner direction. As when he says:

> If the world market begins to fall apart under pressures that it can no longer contain, Europe will be the largest economic bloc. Its size and wealth will enable it to press for reforms limiting the mobility of capital ...
>
> The free market has never had in Europe the commanding position it has sometimes exercised in English-speaking countries. It is not inconceivable that

the European Union could take the lead in building a new framework for the world economy in the wake of the collapse of global *laissez-faire.* [11]

The hope that Gray holds out expresses itself politically in terms of the tolerant, pluralist liberal and democratic ideal championed by thinkers like Isaiah Berlin and Richard Rorty, chastened by a Postmodernist distrust of "grand narratives", and tinged with a conservative respect for "organic communities" and their traditions. Gray's hope expresses itself economically in terms of an implicit appeal to something like "global Keynesianism" - to something like the managed framework for the world economy which Keynes hoped to see set up at the Bretton Woods Conference, only in the contemporary case a management more concerned with something like global planning in regard to pressing issues of resources, population, pollution, and sustainable global development. This would be a world where there would be a balance between global planning and (controlled) market activity with respect for indigenous cultures and their own preferred political/ economic organization.

On some understandings, this would be a kind of "centralization within decentralization" which Karl Marx, with his reluctance to provide "blueprints for utopia", might almost have approved of.

Notes

1. K. Marx and F. Engels, *The Communist Manifesto*, Penguin, 1987, pp. 104-105.
2. J. Schumpeter, *Capitalism, Socialism and Democracy*, pp. 261-262.
3. J. Schumpeter, Ibid, p. 116.
4. Jean-Jacques Rousseau, *The Social Contract*, trans. M. Cranston, Penguin, 1968, p. 96, ftn.
5. John Gray, *False Dawn: The Delusions of Global Capitalism*, Granta, 1998, pp. 211-218.
6. J. Gray, Ibid., p. 210.
7. J. Gray, Ibid., pp. 210-211.
8. J. Gray, Ibid., p. 200.

9. J. Gray, Ibid., p. 199.
10. J. Gray, Ibid., pp. 207-208.
11. J. Gray, Ibid., pp. 233-234.

Bibliography

Arlblaster, A. and Lukes, S. (1971) *The Good Society*, Methuen.

Barratt Brown, M. (1990) *Models in Political Economy*, Penguin.

Brenner, R. (1998) *The Economics of Global Turbulence*, N.L.R.

Callinicos, A. (1984) *The Revolutionary Road to Socialism*, S.W.P.

Carew Hunt, R.N. (1950) *The Theory and Practice of Communism*, Penguin.

Dalton, G. (1983) *Economic Systems and Society*, Penguin.

Engels, F. (1907) *Socialism: Utopian and Scientific*, Swan Sonnenschein & Co., London.

Galbraith, J.K. (1971) *The Affluent Society*, Penguin.

Galbraith, J.K. (1991) *A History of Economics*, Penguin.

Galbraith, J.K. and Salinger, N. (1978) *Almost Everyone's Guide to Economics*, Penguin.

Gorz, Andre (1989) *Critique of Economic Reason*, Verso.

Gray, J. (1996) *After Social Democracy*, Demos.

Gray, J. (1998) *False Dawn: the Delusions of Global Capitalism*, Granta.

Harrington, M. (1993) *Socialism: Past and Future*, Pluto Press.

Hegel, G.W.F. (1967) *Philosophy of Right*, Oxford U.P.

Hegel, G.W.F. (1977) *The Phenomenology of Spirit*, Oxford U.P.

Heilbroner, R. (1953) *The Worldly Philosophers*, Penguin.

Heilbroner, R. (1995) *Visions of the Future*, Oxford U.P.

Heilbroner, R. and Thurow, L. (1994) *Economics Explained*, Simon & Schuster.

Ignatieff, M. (1998) *The Warrior's Honor*, Chatto & Windus.

Lichteim, G. (1961) *Marxism*, Routledge.

Marshall, A. (1961) *Principles of Economics*, Vol. 1, Macmillan.

Marx, K. (1962) *Marx on Economics* (ed.) R. Freedman, Penguin.
Marx, K. (1973) *Grundrisse*, Allen Lane.
Marx, K. (1976, 1978, 1981) *Capital*, Vols. 1-3 (ed.) E. Mandel, Penguin.
Marx, K. and Engels, F. (1987) *The Communist Manifesto*, Penguin.
Marx, K. and Engels, F. (1989) *The German Ideology*, Lawrence & Wishart.
Morton, A.L. (1969) *The English Utopia*, Lawrence & Wishart.
O.E.C.D. (1998) *Twenty First Century Technology*, O.E.C.D.
Rifkin, J. (1995) *The End of Work*, J.P. Tarcher/G.P. Putnam, N.Y.
Rousseau, J.-J. (1968) *The Social Contract*, Penguin.
Schumpeter, J. (1987) *Capitalism, Socialism and Democracy*, George Allen & Unwin.
Weil, S. (1952) *Gravity and Grace*, Routledge & Kegan Paul.
Weil, S. (1972) *Oppression and Liberty*, Routledge & Kegan Paul.
Wilson, E. (1960) *To the Finland Station*, W.H. Allen.

Index